A DAY
WITH THE
PROPHET

AHMAD VON DENFFER

THE ISLAMIC FOUNDATION

A day with the Prophet ﷺ

Published by
THE ISLAMIC FOUNDATION,
Markfield Conference Centre, Ratby Lane,
Markfield, Leicestershire, LE67 9SY, UK
E-mail: publications@islamic-foundation.com
Website: www.islamic-foundation.com

Quran House, P.O. Box 30611, Nairobi, Kenya

PMB 3196, Kano, Nigeria

Distributed by
KUBE PUBLISHING LTD.
Tel: +44(0)1530 249230, Fax: +44(0)1530 249656
E-mail: info@kubepublishing.com

Cataloguing-in-Publication Data is available
from the British Library

ISBN 978-0- 86037-121-2

Typeset by: N.A. Qaddoura
Cover design by: Imran Khan
Printed by: Imak Ofset, Turkey

عَنِ الْـحَسَنِ ﷺ قَالَ: لَـمَّا بَعَثَ اللهُ مُحَمَّدًا ﷺ قَالَ: هَذَا نَبِيٌّ، هَذَا خَيَارَى، ائْنَسُوا بِهِ وَخُذُوا فِي سُنَّتِهِ وَسَبِيلِهِ، لَمْ يَكُنْ تُغْلَقُ دُونَهُ الأَبْوَابُ وَلَا يَقُومُ دُونَهُ الْـحَجَبَةُ وَلَا يُغْدَى عَلَيْهِ بِالْجِفَانِ وَلَا يُرَاحُ عَلَيْهِ بِهَا وَكَانَ يَجْلِسُ بِالأَرْضِ وَيَأْكُلُ طَعَامَهُ بِالأَرْضِ وَيَلْبَسُ الْغَلِيظَ وَيَرْكَبُ الْـحِمَارَ وَيُرْدِفُ عَبْدَهُ وَيَلْعَقُ وَاللهِ أَصَابِعَهُ. وكَانَ يَقُولُ: مَنْ يَرْغَبُ عَنْ سُنَّتِي فَلَيْسَ مِنِّي.

الطَّبَقَاتُ لِابْنِ سَعْدٍ

Ḥasan said that when Allah sent Muḥammad ﷺ, He said: 'This is My Prophet, this is My chosen one; love him, and adopt his *Sunnah* and his path. Doors are not locked up under him, nor do doorkeepers stand for him, and trays of food are not served to him in the morning or the evening, but he sits on the ground and eats his food from the ground. He wears coarse clothes and rides on a donkey, with others sitting behind him, and he licks his fingers (after taking food). He says: "He who does not like my *Sunnah*, does not belong to me."'

Ṭabaqāt Ibn Saʿd

Transliteration Table

Arabic Consonants

Initial, unexpressed medial and final: ء ’

ا a	د d	ض ḍ	ك k
ب b	ذ dh	ط ṭ	ل l
ت t	ر r	ظ ẓ	م m
ث th	ز z	ع ‘	ن n
ج j	س s	غ gh	هـ h
ح ḥ	ش sh	ف f	و w
خ kh	ص ṣ	ق q	ي y

With a *shaddah*, both medial and final consonants are doubled.

Vowels, diphthongs, etc.

Short:	a ـَ	i ـِ	u ـُ
Long:	ā ـَا	ī ـِي	ū ـُو
Diphthongs:		ـَوْ aw	
		ـَىْ ay	

Contents

Foreword

For most of us, an ordinary day is pretty uneventful, yet the quality of our everyday life is crucially important to our peace and happiness. Living that life can be a pleasure and a joy, but it can also be a burden and a misery or, quite simply, a boring and meaningless exercise. It all depends on how we live each day: with what inner attitudes we approach it, and with what outward actions we fill its hours. Living we cannot escape, and deep within us lies a constant longing search for a life of joy and meaning. This longing quest has gained an extra dimension in our time, as manifest in our preoccupation with what we call 'lifestyle'. But though a new 'style' comes into vogue almost daily, the real 'life' in living remains as elusive as ever.

We may be surprised, therefore, to find new vistas opening before us when we follow the Prophet Muḥammad (peace be upon him) through an ordinary day, observing the lifestyle he practised and offered as an example to others. By sketching a typical day in the Prophet's life, this small book invites us to follow that very lifestyle. It is obvious that no book, and certainly not one of this size, could ever succeed in conveying fully and faithfully the rich and perfect life lived by the Prophet. Nevertheless, I hope that what my colleague, Brother Ahmad von Denffer, has achieved in this direction will inspire many to follow in the footsteps of the Prophet: 'the best and the finest model for us' (*al-Aḥzab* 33: 21), and 'a mercy for the whole of mankind' (*al-Anbiyā'* 21: 107).

It may be helpful to draw attention to what I see as one of the most remarkable inner dimensions of the Prophet's lifestyle, though no-one could hope to do full justice to this important aspect of his life. What strikes me as most significant, apart from his simplicity, is his total freedom from servitude to any created thing, especially to external physical objects and to false internal notions. What joy such a liberation should bring to man! Especially when we know that the lot of the average man is to toil and grind under artificial yokes from the cradle to the grave.

In an age whose *Weltanschauung* takes account only of the physical objects that surround man, but have no true or abiding relationship or value for him, a whole new meaning and outlook is imparted by the Prophet's lifestyle. Every ordinary activity is oriented towards God, not by taking us away from the chores of daily life, but by making God the very core of that life and existence. Life is no longer an abysmal darkness, with a past shaped by the blind force of chance and staring into a future without hope of meaning. Instead, every word and deed from morning till evening is firmly rooted in our origins and looks forward to a glorious future. What a blessing this must be! What peace this must bring!

I hope that all who read this book will accept the author's invitation and try to live at least one day as the Prophet himself lived it. There can be no greater blessing than a day lived in peace and harmony. The Islamic Foundation plans to bring out a series of books on various aspects of the Prophet's life on the occasion of the *Hijra* Centenary. This book is one of them. We realise that no effort can adequately communicate to our age the meaning and message of the Prophet's life, but we pray to Allah to enable us to do whatever we can towards the fulfilment of this great task. I also pray to Him to bless our humble efforts with His acceptance and grace.

The Islamic Foundation **Khurram Jah Murad**
Leicester Director General
1 *Dhū al-Qaʿdah* 1399
23 September 1979

Introduction

Many Muslims are well acquainted with the *Sunnah* of the Prophet as a *terminus technicus* and all that it stands for in Muslim history and legal thought. How many though, one wonders, try to model their lives on the *Sunnah*, every day, from morning till night? The almost complete adoption of the 'modern', that is, Western way of life by many people of Muslim origin suggests that the number is small indeed.

Nevertheless, it is accepted among Muslims that the *Sunnah* is the key to understanding the message of the Holy Qur'ān and to the implementation of the guidelines and laws laid down in it. While revealed scripture explains the basic principles and laws of Islam as a way of life, the *Sunnah* teaches Islam through explanation and demonstration of those principles and laws; it makes them part of man's experience by showing how they work in practice. The *Sunnah* is thus indispensable if one wants to practise Islam and be a true Muslim. It is in this sense that the Holy Qur'ān states:

> 'He who obeys the Messenger has obeyed Allah...' (*al-Nisā'* 4: 80)

Thus whether or not to follow the *Sunnah* has not been left to the discretion of the Muslim, and to practise Islam on the lines given by the Prophet himself has been made an obligation, as the Qur'ān says:

> 'And whatever the Messenger gives you, accept it, and whatever he forbids you, abstain (from it)...' (*al-Ḥashr* 59: 7)

Bearing this in mind, the following pages are meant as an invitation, to Muslims and non-Muslims alike, to consider leading their lives according to the *Sunnah* of the Prophet.

For many reasons this may seem to be too difficult a task. To live by the *Sunnah* would certainly make a difference: but whether it is in fact more difficult to live by God-given rules than by the man-imposed and alienating patterns and norms of behaviour that are at the basis of today's way of life, can only be discovered if one tries it for oneself.

To adopt a different lifestyle is naturally something that takes time, something that one has to grow into. Nevertheless, why not just try spending a day with the Prophet? Observe the rules and norms presented in this introductory selection of *aḥādīth* for a full day, from rising in the early morning to going to sleep late at night.

See what it means to you to get up in the morning and to remember Allah and His Messenger in your first thoughts and action. Spend the morning with the Prophet, doing as he did in your activities. Spend the afternoon likewise; then the evening and then the night. Think of Allah and His Messenger before going to sleep, and think about your day, this one day you have tried to live by the *Sunnah*. Think about it and ask yourself whether it has simply been too difficult, or whether by the grace of Allah you have benefited from it. And then think about spending the coming day, too, with the Prophet.

The *aḥādīth* presented here have been selected and translated from the accepted collections of *Ṣaḥīḥ al-Bukhārī, Ṣaḥīḥ Muslim, Jāmiʿ al-Tirmidhī, Abī Dāwūd, Sunan al-Nasāʾī* and *Sunan lbn Mājah*. A number of them were taken from the *Mishkāt al-Maṣābīḥ* and *Riyāḍ al-Ṣāliḥīn*. Occasionally a footnote has been added to clarify a point. The translation is not always in exact English. Rather, I have aimed at conveying the meaning while keeping close to the words and structure of the Arabic phrases.

The customary blessings on the Prophet in the Arabic original each time his name is mentioned have not been repeated in the translations, but the reader is kindly requested to observe this Muslim tradition.

Last, but not least, I should mention that the book in its present form owes much to the kind advice of Khurram Jah Murad. He read the first draft and made a number of suggestions for improvement, most of which I gladly incorporated when finalizing the script. May Allah reward him. May Allah accept this humble effort; and may Allah bless those who try to follow the *Sunnah* of His Messenger.

Leicester   **Ahmad von Denffer**
Ramaḍān 1399
July 1979

1

To Begin in the Name of Allah

———————————

لِقَوْلِهِ ﷺ: كُلُّ كَلَامٍ لَا يُبْدَأُ فِيهِ بِبِسْمِ اللهِ الرَّحْمَنِ الرَّحِيمِ فَهُوَ أَجْذَمُ.

تَفْسِيرُ ابن كَثِيرٍ

1 According to the word of the Prophet ﷺ: 'Any activity not begun with the words "In the Name of Allah, the Beneficent, the Merciful"'[1] is severed (from its blessings).

Tafsīr Ibn Kathīr

———————————

[1] Arabic: *Bismi-llāhi-r-raḥmāni-r-raḥīm*

Regular Deeds

عَـنْ عَائِشَةَ ﷺ قَالَتْ: قَالَ رَسُــولُ اللهِ ﷺ: إِنَّ أَحَبَّ الأَعْمَـالِ عِنْدَ اللهِ أَدْوَمُهَا وَإِنْ قَلَّ.

مُتَّفَقٌ عَلَيْهِ

2 'Ā'ishah ﷺ said that Allah's Messenger ﷺ said: 'The deeds most loved by Allah (are those) done regularly, even if they are small.'

Bukhārī, Muslim

3

Waking up at Night and Rising in the Early Morning

عَنْ مَسْرُوقٍ ﷺ قَالَ: سَأَلْتُ عَائِشَةَ ﷺ: أَيُّ الْعَمَلِ كَانَ
أَحَبَّ إِلَى النَّبِيِّ ﷺ؟ قَالَتِ: الدَّائِمُ قَالَ: قُلْتُ: فَأَيُّ حِينٍ
كَانَ يَقُومُ؟ قَالَتْ: كَانَ يَقُومُ إِذَا سَمِعَ الصَّارِخَ.

مُتَّفَقٌ عَلَيْهِ

3 Masrūq ﷺ said: 'I asked 'Ā'ishah ﷺ: "Which action was most loved by Allah's Prophet ﷺ?" She said: "The one regularly done." I said: "When did he get up at night?" She said: "He got up at cockcrow."'

Bukhārī, Muslim

عَنْ عَائِشَـةَ ﴿رضي الله عنها﴾ أَنَّ النَّبِيَّ ﷺ كَانَ يَنَامُ أَوَّلَ اللَّيْلِ ويَقُومُ آخِرَهُ فَيُصَلِّي.

مُتَّفَقٌ عَلَيْه

4 'Ā'ishah ﷺ said that the Prophet ﷺ used to sleep during the earlier part of the night and stood praying during the latter part.

Bukhārī, Muslim

———— ∞∞∞ ————

عَنْ أَبِي هُرَيْرَةَ ﴿رضي الله عنه﴾ قَالَ: سَمِعْتُ رَسُولَ الله ﷺ يَقُولُ: إِنَّ أَفْضَلَ الصَّلاةِ بَعْدَ الْـمَفْرُوضَةِ الصَّلاةُ فِي جَوْفِ اللَّيْلِ.

رَوَاهُ أَحْمَد

5 Abū Huraira ﷺ said that he heard Allah's Messenger ﷺ say: 'The best prayer after the obligatory one is the prayer in the middle of the night.'

Aḥmad

———— ∞∞∞ ————

عَنْ أَبِي أُمَامَةَ ﴿رضي الله عنه﴾ قَالَ: قَالَ رَسُولُ الله ﷺ: عَلَيْكُمْ بِقِيَامِ اللَّيْلِ فَإِنَّهُ دَأْبُ الصَّالِحِينَ قَبْلَكُمْ وَهُوَ قُرْبَةٌ إِلَى رَبِّكُمْ وَمَكْفَرَةٌ لِلسَّيِّئَاتِ وَمَنْهَاةٌ لِلإِثْمِ.

رَوَاهُ التِّرْمِذِيُّ

6 Abū Umāma ﷺ said that Allah's Messenger ﷺ said: 'Getting up at night is enjoined upon you, for it was the practice of the pious before you. It brings you near to your Lord and is an atonement for evil deeds and a restraint from sins.'

Tirmidhī

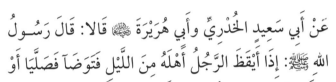

عَنْ أَبِي سَعِيدٍ الْخُدْرِيِّ وأَبِي هُرَيْرَةَ ﵁ قَالَا: قَالَ رَسُـولُ اللهِ ﷺ: إِذَا أَيْقَظَ الرَّجُلُ أَهْلَهُ مِنَ اللَّيْلِ فَتَوَضَّأَ فَصَلَّيَا أَوْ صَلَّى رَكْعَتَيْنِ جَمِيعًا كُتِبَا فِي الذَّاكِرِينَ وَالذَّاكِرَاتِ.

رَوَاهُ أَبُو دَاوُدَ وَابْنُ مَاجَهْ

7 Abū Saʿīd and Abū Huraira ﷺ said that Allah's Messenger ﷺ said: 'When a man wakes up his wife at night and they pray two *rakʿa*[1] together, they are written down among the men and women who remember Allah.'

Abū Dāwūd, Ibn Mājah

---

[1] The prescribed prayers (Arabic: *ṣalāt*) consist of a fixed number of such sections.

عَنْ أَبِي هُرَيْرَةَ ﷺ قَالَ: قَالَ رَسُولُ الله ﷺ: يَعْقِدُ الشَّيْطَانُ عَلَى قَافِيَةِ رَأْسِ أَحَدِكُمْ ثَلَاثَ عُقَدٍ إِذَا نَامَ بِكُلِّ عُقْدَةٍ يَضْرِبُ: عَلَيْكَ لَيْلًا طَوِيلًا، فَإِذَا اسْتَيْقَظَ فَذَكَرَ اللهَ انْحَلَّتْ عُقْدَةٌ وَإِذَا تَوَضَّأَ انْحَلَّتْ عَنْهُ عُقْدَتَانِ فَإِذَا صَلَّى انْحَلَّتِ الْعُقَدُ فَأَصْبَحَ نَشِيطًا طَيِّبَ النَّفْسِ وَإِلَّا أَصْبَحَ خَبِيثَ النَّفْسِ كَسْلَانَ.

مُتَّفَقٌ عَلَيْهِ

8 Abū Huraira ﷺ said that Allah's Messenger ﷺ said: 'When one of you sleeps, *Shaiṭān*[2] ties three knots at the back of his neck, and closes each knot with (the words): "You have a long night, so sleep". When one wakes up and remembers Allah, the first knot is untied; when one performs ablution, the second is untied; and when one prays, the third is untied; and one starts the day energetically and in good spirits. Otherwise, one will begin the morning in a bad humour, and full of sloth.'

Bukhārī, Muslim

---

[2] The Evil One (Satan).

وعَنْ حُذَيْفَةَ ﵁ قَالَ: كَانَ النَّبِيُّ ﷺ إِذَا أَخَذَ مَضْجَعَهُ
مِنَ اللَّيْلِ وَضَعَ يَدَهُ تَحْتَ خَدِّهِ ، ثُمَّ يَقُولُ : اللَّهُمَّ بِاسْمِكَ
أَمُوتُ وَ أَحْيَا. وإِذَا اسْتَيْقَظَ قَالَ: الْـحَمْدُ لله اَلَّذِي أَحْيَانَا
بَعْدَ مَا أَمَاتَنَا وإِلَيْهِ النُّشُورُ.

رَوَاهُ الْبُخَارِيُّ

9 Ḥudhaifa ﵁ said that the Prophet ﷺ, when he lay
down at night, used to place his hand under his
cheek and then say: 'O Allah, in Your name I die and
live'[3] and when he woke up, he said: 'All praise be to
Allah Who gave us life, after He had given us death,
and to Him is the return.'[4]

Bukhārī

عَنْ عَائِشَةَ ﵂ قَالَتْ: كَانَ النَّبِيُّ ﷺ إِذَا قَامَ مِنَ اللَّيْلِ
لِيُصَلِّيَ افْتَتَحَ صَلَاتَهُ بِرَكْعَتَيْنِ خَفِيفَتَيْنِ.

رَوَاهُ مُسْلِمٌ

---

[3] Arabic: *Allahumma bismika amūtu wa aḥyā.*
[4] Arabic: *Al-ḥamdu li-llāhi ladhī aḥyānā baʿda mā amātanā wa
ilaihi-n-nushūr.*

10 'Ā'ishah ⁓ said that Allah's Messenger ⁓, when he got up at night, opened his prayer with two short *rak'as.*

Muslim

عَنْ عَبْدِ اللهِ بْنِ عَبَّاسٍ ⁓ أَنَّهُ رَقَدَ عِنْدَ رَسُولِ اللهِ ⁓ فَاسْتَيْقَظَ فَتَسَوَّكَ وَتَوَضَّأَ وَهُوَ يَقُولُ: «إِنَّ فِي خَلْقِ السَّمَـٰوَاتِ وَالأَرْضِ وَاخْتِلَافِ اللَّيْلِ وَالنَّهَارِ لَآيَاتٍ لِأُولِي الأَلْبَابِ ...». فَقَرَأَ هَؤُلَاءِ الآيَاتِ حَتَّى خَتَمَ السُّورَةَ. ثُمَّ قَامَ فَصَلَّى رَكْعَتَيْنِ فَأَطَالَ فِيهِمَا القِيَامَ وَالرُّكُوعَ وَالسُّجُودَ. ثُمَّ انْصَرَفَ فَنَامَ حَتَّى نَفَخَ ثُمَّ فَعَلَ ذَلِكَ ثَلَاثَ مَرَّاتٍ سِتَّ رَكَعَاتٍ. كُلُّ ذَلِكَ يَسْتَاكُ وَيَتَوَضَّأُ وَيَقْرَأُ هَؤُلَاءِ الآيَاتِ ثُمَّ أَوْتَرَ بِثَلَاثٍ فَأَذَّنَ الـمُؤَذِّنُ فَخَرَجَ إِلَى الصَّلَاةِ وَهُوَ يَقُولُ: اللَّهُمَّ اجْعَلْ فِي قَلْبِي نُورًا وَفِي لِسَانِي نُورًا وَاجْعَلْ فِي سَمْعِي نُورًا وَاجْعَلْ فِي بَصَرِي نُورًا وَاجْعَلْ مِنْ خَلْفِي نُورًا وَمِنْ أَمَامِي نُورًا وَاجْعَلْ مِنْ فَوْقِي نُورًا وَمِنْ تَحْتِي نُورًا، اللَّهُمَّ أَعْطِنِي نُورًا.

رَوَاهُ مُسْلِمٌ

11 'Abdullāh b. 'Abbās ﷺ said: He slept at the Prophet's house and the Prophet ﷺ got up, brushed his teeth, made ablution and said: 'In the creation of the heavens and the earth and in the alternation of night and day are signs for people of understanding,'[5] and he read those verses till the end of the *sūrah*.[6] Then he stood up and prayed two *rak'a*, prolonging his standing, bowing and prostrating. Then he stopped, and slept deeply. This he did three times, six *rak'a* altogether, brushing his teeth, making ablution and reading those verses every time. Then he performed *witr* with three *rak'a*. Then the *mu'adhdhin*[7] called *adhān*[8] and he went out for prayer, saying: 'O Allah, put Light in my heart and Light in my tongue, put Light in my hearing, put Light in my seeing, put Light behind me and Light in front of me, and put Light above me and Light below me. O Allah, give me Light.'[9]

Muslim

---

[5] *Āl 'Imrān* 3: 190.

[6] Chapter of the Qur'ān. The Qur'ān has 114 *sūrah* or 'chapters'.

[7] The person who calls for prayer at the prescribed time.

[8] The call for prayer.

[9] Arabic: *Allahumma-j'al fī qalbī nūran wa fī lisānī nūran wa-j'al fī sam'ī nūran wa-j'al fī baṣarī nūran wa-j'al fī khalfī nūran wa min amāmī, nūran wa-j'al min fawqī nūran wa min taḥtī nūran, allahumma a'ṭinī nūran.*

4

The Use of the
Right Hand

عَنْ عَائِشَةَ ﷺ قَالَتْ: كَانَتْ يَدُّ رَسُولِ اللهِ ﷺ الْيُمْنَى
لِطُهُـورِهِ وطَعَامِهِ وَكَانَتْ يَدُهُ الْيُسْرَى لِـخَلائِهِ ومَا كَانَ
مِنْ أَذًى.

رَوَاهُ أَبُو دَاوُدَ

12 'Ā'ishah ﷺ said that the right hand was used by Allah's Messenger ﷺ for his ablution and for taking food, and his left hand was used in the toilet and the like.

Abū Dāwūd

The Call of Nature

عَنْ أَنَسِ بْنِ مَالِكٍ ﷺ قَالَ: كَانَ رَسُولُ اللهِ ﷺ إِذَا دَخَلَ الْخَلاءَ قَالَ: اللَّهُمَّ إِنِّي أَعُوذُ بِكَ مِنَ الْخُبْثِ والخَبَائِثِ.

مُتَفَقٌ عَلَيْه

13 Anas b. Mālik ﷺ said that Allah's Messenger ﷺ, when he entered the toilet, used to say: 'O Allah, I seek refuge in You from all kinds of evils.'[1]

Bukhārī, Muslim

عَنْ عَائِشَةَ ﷺ قَالَتْ: كَانَ النَّبِيُّ ﷺ إِذَا خَرَجَ مِنَ الْخَلاءِ قَالَ: غُفْرَانَكَ.

رَوَاهُ التِّرْمِذِيُّ وابْنُ مَاجَه

---

[1] Arabic: *Allahumma innī aʿūdhu bika mina l Khubthi wa l Khabāʾith.*

14 'Ā'ishah ❀ said that the Prophet ﷺ, when he came out of the toilet, used to say: 'Grant Your forgiveness.'[2]

Tirmidhī, Ibn Mājah

❦

عَنْ أَبِي هُرَيْرَةَ ﵁ قَالَ: قَالَ رَسُولُ اللهِ ﷺ: ... ومَنْ أَتَى
الْغَائِطَ فَلْيَسْتَتِرْ.

رَوَاهُ أَبُو دَاوُدَ

15 Abū Huraira ❀ said: The Prophet ﷺ said: '... He who relieves himself, should be concealed (from the view of others) ...'

Abū Dāwūd

❦

عَنْ أَبِي سَعِيدٍ ﵁ قَالَ: قَالَ رَسُولُ اللهِ ﷺ: لَا يَخْرُج
الرَّجُلَانِ يَضْرِبَانِ الْغَائِطَ كَاشِفَيْنِ عَنْ عَوْرَتِهِمَا يَتَحَدَّثَانِ
فَإِنَّ اللهَ عَزَّ وَجَلَّ يَمْقُتُ عَلَى ذَلِكَ.

رَوَاهُ أَبُو دَاوُدَ وَابْنُ مَاجَه

---

[2] Arabic: *ghufrānak*.

16 Abū Saʿīd ﷺ said that Allah's Messenger ﷺ said: 'Two people should not go out together to relieve themselves, uncovering their private parts and talking to each other, for Allah abhors this.'

Abū Dāwūd, Ibn Mājah

عَنْ عُمَرَ ﵁ قَالَ: رَآنِي النَّبِيُّ ﷺ وَأَنَا أَبُولُ قَائِمًا فَقَالَ: يَا عُمَرُ! لَا تَبُلْ قَائِمًا! فَمَا بُلْتُ قَائِمًا بَعْدُ.

رَوَاهُ التِّرْمِذِيُّ

17 ʿUmar ﷺ said: The Prophet ﷺ saw me passing water while standing. He said: 'O ʿUmar, do not pass water while standing.' So after that I did not pass water while standing.

Tirmidhī

عَنْ أَبِي هُرَيْرَةَ ﵁ قَالَ: كَانَ النَّبِيُّ ﷺ إِذَا أَتَى الْخَلَاءَ أَتَيْتُهُ بِمَاءٍ فِي تَوْرٍ أَوْ رَكْوَةٍ فَاسْتَنْجَى ثُمَّ مَسَحَ يَدَهُ عَلَى الْأَرْضِ، ثُمَّ أَتَيْتُهُ بِإِنَاءٍ آخَرَ فَتَوَضَّأَ.

رَوَاهُ أَبُو دَاوُدَ

18 Abū Huraira ﷺ said that when the Prophet ﷺ went to the toilet he[3] brought him water in a container or a skin, and he[4] cleansed himself. Then he[3] wiped his hand on the ground. Then he[3] brought him another container, and he[4] made ablution.

Abū Dāwūd

Ablution

وعَنْ حُذَيْفَةَ ﷺ قَـالَ: كَانَ النَّبِيُّ ﷺ إذا قَـامَ لِلتَّهَجُّدِ مِنَ اللَّيْلِ يَشُوصُ فَاهُ بِالسِّوَاكِ.

مُتَّفَقٌ عَلَيْهِ

19 Ḥudhaifa ﷺ said that Allah's Messenger ﷺ, when he got up from sleep, for *tahajjud* prayer, cleansed his mouth with a *siwāk*.

Bukhārī, Muslim

وعَنْ عُثْمَانَ بْنِ عَفَّانَ ﷺ قَـالَ: قَالَ رَسُـولُ الله ﷺ: مَنْ تَوَضَّأَ فَأَحْسَنَ الوُضُوءَ خَرَجَتْ خَطَايَاهُ مِنْ جَسَدِهِ حَتَّى تَخْرُجُ مِنْ تَحْتِ أَظْفَارِهِ.

رَوَاهُ مُسْلِم

20 'Uthmān b. 'Affān said that Allah's Messenger ﷺ said: 'He who makes ablution and makes it in the best way, his sins leave his body, even from beneath his nails.'

Muslim

7

Bathing

عَنْ عَائِشَةَ ﷺ زَوْجِ النَّبِيِّ ﷺ أَنَّ النَّبِيَّ ﷺ كَانَ إِذَا اغْتَسَلَ مِنَ الْجَنَابَةِ بَدَأَ فَغَسَلَ يَدَيْهِ ثُمَّ يَتَوَضَّأُ كَمَا يَتَوَضَّأُ لِلصَّلاةِ، ثُمَّ يُدْخِلُ أَصَابِعَهُ فِي الْمَاءِ فَيُخَلِّلُ بِهَا أُصُولَ شَعْرِهِ ثُمَّ يَصُبُّ عَلَى رَأْسِهِ ثَلاثَ غُرَفٍ بِيَدِهِ ثُمَّ يُفِيضُ الْمَاءَ عَلَى جِلْدِهِ كُلِّهِ. رَوَاهُ الْبُخَارِيُّ

21 'Ā'ishah, the wife of the Prophet, said: 'Usually the Prophet, when bathing because of *janaba*,[1] began by washing his hands. Then he made ablution as for prayer. Then he put his fingers in water and ran them through the roots of his hair and then poured three handfuls of water with his hands over his head, and then let the water flow all over his body.'

---

[1] The state of ritual impurity after sexual intercourse or wet dreams (*iḥtilām*).

عَنْ أَبِي هُرَيْرَةَ ﷺ قَالَ: قَالَ رَسُولُ الله ﷺ: حَقَّ عَلَى كُلِّ مُسْـلِمٍ أَنْ يَغْتَسِلَ فِي كُلِّ سَـبْعَةِ أَيَّامٍ يَوْمًا يَغْسِلُ فِيـهِ رَأْسَهُ وَجَسَدَهُ.

مُتَّفَقٌ عَلَيْهِ

22 Abū Huraira ﷺ said that Allah's Messenger ﷺ said: 'It is an obligation on every Muslim to bath (at least once) every seven days and wash both his head and body.'

Bukhārī, Muslim

8

Early Morning Prayer

عَنْ جَابِر ﷺ قَالَ : قَالَ رَسُولُ الله ﷺ: إِنَّ في اللَّيْل سَاعَةً
لا يُوَافِقُهَا رَجُلٌ مُسْلِمٌ يَسْأَلُ اللهَ تَعَالَى فِيهَا خَيْرًا مِنْ أَمْرِ
الدُّنْيَا وَالآخِرَةِ إِلَّا أَعْطَاهُ إِيَّاهُ ، وَذَلِكَ كُلُّ لَيْلَةٍ.

رَوَاهُ مُسْلِم

23 Jābir ﷺ said that he heard Allah's Messenger ﷺ say: 'At night there is a time when there is no Muslim who stays up and asks Allah the Good of this world and the Hereafter without it being granted to him, and such a time is every night.'

Muslim

عَـنِ ابْنِ عُمَرَ ﷺ قَـالَ: كَانَ النَّبِيُّ ﷺ يُصَلِّي مِـنَ اللَّيْل
مَثْـنَى مَثْنَى وِيُوتِرُ بِرَكْعَةٍ.

رَوَاهُ الْبُخَارِيُّ

24 Ibn 'Umar ﷺ said: At night the Prophet ﷺ used to pray *rak'as* in two's and then (finished with) one.

Bukhārī

عَنْ أَبِي هُرَيْرَةَ ﵁ قَالَ: كَانَتْ قِرَاءَةُ النَّبِيِّ ﷺ بِاللَّيْلِ يَرْفَعُ صَوْتَهُ طَوْرًا وَيَخْفِضُ طَوْرًا.

رَوَاهُ أَبُو دَاوُدَ

25 Abū Huraira ﷺ said that Allah's Messenger's ﷺ reading (of the prayer) at night used to be (at times) with a loud voice and at times with a soft voice.

Abū Dāwūd

9

Daily Prayers

عَنْ أَبِي هُرَيْرَةَ رَضِيَ اللهُ أَنَّهُ سَمِعَ رَسُولَ اللهِ ﷺ يَقُولُ: أَرَأَيْتُمْ لَوْ
أَنَّ نَهْرًا بِبَابِ أَحَدِكُمْ يَغْتَسِلُ مِنْهُ كُلَّ يَوْمٍ خَمْسَ مَرَّاتٍ هَلْ
يَبْقَى مِنْ دَرَنِهِ شَيْءٌ؟ قَالُوا: لَا يَبْقَى مِنْ دَرَنِهِ شَيْءٌ. قَالَ:
فَذَلِكَ مَثَلُ الصَّلَوَاتِ الْخَمْسِ يَمْحُو اللهُ بِهِنَّ الْخَطَايَا.
رَوَاهُ الْبُخَارِيُّ

26 Abū Huraira ؓ heard Allah's Messenger ﷺ say: 'If there was a river at the door of (the house of) one of you, and he bathed in it every day five times, would you say that any dirt would be left on him?' They said: 'No dirt at all would be left on him.' He said: 'That is the example of the five prayers by which Allah washes away sins.'

Bukhārī

وَعَنْ عَبْدِ اللهِ بْنِ مَسْعُودٍ ﷺ قَالَ: سَأَلْتُ النَّبِيَّ ﷺ: أَيُّ الْعَمَلِ أَحَبُّ إِلَى اللهِ؟ قَالَ: الصَّلَاةُ عَلَى وَقْتِهَا.

رَوَاهُ الْبُخَارِيُّ

27 'Abdullāh b. Mas'ud ﷺ said that he asked the Prophet ﷺ which deed was loved most by Allah, the Exalted. He said: 'Prayer which is performed at its time.'

Bukhārī

عَنِ ابْنِ عَبَّاسٍ ﷺ قَالَ: قَالَ رَسُولُ اللهِ ﷺ: أَمَّنِي جِبْرِيلُ عِنْدَ الْبَيْتِ مَرَّتَيْنِ، فَصَلَّى بِيَ الظُّهْرَ حِينَ زَالَتِ الشَّمْسُ فَكَانَ كَقَدْرِ الشِّرَاكِ، ثُمَّ صَلَّى بِيَ الْعَصْرَ حِينَ صَارَ ظِلُّ كُلِّ شَيْءٍ مِثْلَهُ، ثُمَّ صَلَّى بِيَ الْمَغْرِبَ حِينَ أَفْطَرَ الصَّائِمُ، ثُمَّ صَلَّى بِيَ الْعِشَاءَ حِينَ غَابَ الشَّفَقُ، ثُمَّ صَلَّى بِيَ الْفَجْرَ حِينَ حَرُمَ الطَّعَامُ وَالشَّرَابُ عَلَى الصَّائِمِ، ثُمَّ صَلَّى بِيَ الظُّهْرَ مِنَ الْغَدِ حِينَ صَارَ ظِلُّ كُلِّ شَيْءٍ مِثْلَهُ، ثُمَّ صَلَّى بِيَ الْعَصْرَ حِينَ صَارَ ظِلُّ كُلِّ شَيْءٍ مِثْلَيْهِ، ثُمَّ صَلَّى بِيَ الْمَغْرِبَ حِينَ أَفْطَرَ الصَّائِمُ، ثُمَّ صَلَّى بِيَ الْعِشَاءَ حِينَ ذَهَبَ ثُلُثُ اللَّيْلِ، ثُمَّ

صَلَّى بِيَ الْفَجْرَ فَأَسْفَرَ، ثُمَّ الْتَفَتَ إِلَيَّ فَقَالَ: يَا مُحَمَّدُ! هَذَا وَقْتُ الأَنْبِيَاءِ قَبْلَكَ، الْوَقْتُ فِيمَا بَيْنَ هَذَيْنِ الْوَقْتَيْنِ .

رَوَاهُ أَبُو دَاوُدَ والتِّرْمِذِيُّ

28 From Ibn 'Abbās ؓ: Allah's Messenger ﷺ said: "Gabriel twice led me (in prayer) at the House[1] and he prayed *zuhr*[2] with me when the sun had declined as far as the strap of a sandal, and he prayed *'asr*[3] with me when the shadows were as long as the things, and he prayed *maghrib*[4] with me when he who fasts breaks (his fast), and he prayed *'ishā'*[5] with me when the twilight had disappeared, and he prayed *fajr*[6] with me (at dawn) when eating and drinking become forbidden for him who fasts. When the next day came, he prayed *zuhr* with me when his shadow was as (long as) he (himself) was, and he prayed *'asr* with me when his shadow was twice as (long as) he (himself) was, and he prayed *maghrib* with me when he who fasts breaks (his fast), and he prayed *'ishā'* with me (after) a third of the night (had passed) and he prayed *fajr* with me when the morning light shone. Then he turned to me and said: "O Muhammad, these are the prayer times of the

---

[1] The *Ka'bah*.
[2] The noon prayer.
[3] The afternoon prayer.
[4] The evening prayer.
[5] The night prayer.
[6] The dawn prayer.

prophets before you, and the time (of each prayer) is
between the two time limits."'

Abū Dāwūd, Tirmidhī

عَنْ أَبِي الدَّرْدَاءِ ﷺ قَالَ: قَالَ رَسُولُ اللهِ ﷺ: مَا مِنْ ثَلَاثَةٍ
فِي قَرْيَةٍ وَلَا بَدْوٍ لَا يُقَامُ فِيهِمُ الصَّلَاةُ إِلَّا اسْتَحْوَذَ عَلَيْهِمُ
الشَّيْطَانُ، فَعَلَيْكُمْ بِالْجَمَاعَةِ، فَإِنَّمَا يَأْكُلُ الذِّئْبُ الْقَاصِيَةَ.

رَوَاهُ أَحْمَدُ وَأَبُو دَاوُدَ

29 Abū al-Dardā' ﷺ said that he heard Allah's Messenger ﷺ say: 'There are not three in a village or of the
desert-people whom, if their prayer is not in *jamā'a*,[7]
Shaitān has (not) already overcome. Thus the *jamā'a*
is enjoined on you, for the wolf eats the solitary
sheep.'

Aḥmad, Abū Dāwūd

عَنِ ابْنِ عُمَرَ ﷺ قَالَ: قَالَ رَسُولُ اللهِ ﷺ: صَلَاةُ الْجَمَاعَةِ
تَفْضُلُ عَلَى صَلَاةِ الْفَرْدِ بِسَبْعٍ وَعِشْرِينَ دَرَجَةً.

مُتَّفَقٌ عَلَيْهِ

---

[7] The congregation prayer.

30 From Ibn ʿUmar ﷺ: Allah's Messenger ﷺ said: 'Prayer in congregation is twenty-seven times better than the prayer performed alone.'

Bukhārī, Muslim

وَعَنْ عُثْمَانَ بنِ عَفَّانَ ﵁ قَالَ: قَالَ رَسُولُ اللهِ ﷺ: مَنْ شَهِدَ العِشَاءَ فِي جَمَاعَةٍ كَانَ لَهُ قِيَامُ نِصْفِ لَيْلَةٍ، ومَنْ صَلَّى العِشَاءَ والفَجْرَ فِي جَمَاعَةٍ، كَانَ لَهُ كَقِيَامِ لَيْلَةٍ.
رَوَاهُ التِّرْمِذِيُّ

31 ʿUthmān b. ʿAffān ﷺ said that Allah's Messenger ﷺ said: 'For him who is present for *ʿishā* in congregation is (the reward of) standing half the night (in prayer), and for him who is present for *ʿishā* and dawn prayer in congregation is (the reward of) standing all night (in prayer).'

Tirmidhī

عَنْ أَبِي قَتَادَةَ السَّلَمِيِّ ﵁ أَنَّ رَسُولَ اللهِ ﷺ قَالَ: إِذَا دَخَلَ أَحَدُكُمُ الْمَسْجِدَ فَلْيَرْكَعْ رَكْعَتَيْنِ قَبْلَ أَنْ يَجْلِسَ.
رَوَاهُ التِّرْمِذِيُّ

32 From Abū Qatāda al-Salamī ⬥: Allah's Messenger ﷺ said: 'When one of you enters the mosque, he should pray two *rak'as* before sitting down.'

Tirmidhī

عن أَبِي هُرَيْرَةَ ﵁ قَالَ: قَالَ رَسُولُ اللهِ ﷺ: إِذَا صَلَّى أَحَدُكُمْ لِلنَّاسِ فَلْيُخَفِّفْ، فَإِنَّ فِيهِمُ الضَّعِيفَ وَالسَّقِيمَ وَذَا الْحَاجَةِ، وَإِذَا صَلَّى أَحَدُكُمْ لِنَفْسِهِ فَلْيُطَوِّلْ مَا شَاءَ.

مُتَّفَقٌ عَلَيْهِ

33 From Abū Huraira ⬥: Allah's Messenger ﷺ said: 'If one of you leads the people in prayer, he should not make it too long, for among them are the sick, the weak and the old; but if one of you prays by himself, he may prolong it as (much as) he wishes.'

Bukhārī, Muslim

عَنْ أَبِي أَيُّوبَ الأَنْصَارِيِّ ﵁ قَالَ: جَاءَ رَجُلٌ إِلَى النَّبِيِّ ﷺ فَقَالَ: عِظْنِي وَأَوْجِزْ، فَقَالَ: إِذَا قُمْتَ فِي صَلَاتِكَ فَصَلِّ صَلَاةَ مُوَدِّعٍ، وَلَا تَكَلَّمْ بِكَلَامٍ تَعْتَذِرُ مِنْهُ غَدًا وَأَجْمِعِ الْيَأْسَ مِمَّا فِي أَيْدِي النَّاسِ.

رَوَاهُ أَحْمَدُ

34 Abū Ayyūb al-Anṣārī ﷺ said that a man came to the Prophet ﷺ and said: 'Give me an advice and make it brief.' He said: 'When you stand up for your prayer, pray as if it was your last prayer; do not say a word for which you will have to make an excuse the coming day, and build no hope on what is at the hands of men.'

Aḥmad

عَنْ ابْنِ عُمَرَ ﵁ قَالَ: قَالَ رَسُــولُ اللهِ ﷺ: اجْعَلُوا فِي بُيُوتِكُمْ مِنْ صَلَاتِكُمْ وَلَا تَتَّخِذُوهَا قُبُورًا.

رَوَاهُ الْبُخَارِيُّ

35 From Ibn 'Umar ﷺ: The Prophet ﷺ said: 'Perform (some) of your prayers at your houses, and do not make them as graves.'

Bukhārī

Supplication

عَنْ أَبِي هُرَيْرَةَ ﷺ قَالَ: قَالَ رَسُولُ اللهِ ﷺ: مَنْ لَمْ يَسْأَلِ اللهَ يَغْضَبْ عَلَيْهِ.

رَوَاهُ التِّرْمِذِيُّ

36 Abū Huraira ﷺ said Allah's Messenger ﷺ said: 'Allah is angry with him who does not ask (anything) from Him.'

Tirmidhī

عَنْ مَالِكِ بْنِ يَسَارٍ ﷺ قَالَ: قَالَ رَسُولُ اللهِ ﷺ: إِذَا سَأَلْتُمُ اللهَ تَعَالَى فَاسْأَلُوهُ بِبُطُونِ أَكُفِّكُمْ ولاَتَسْأَلُوهُ بِظُهُورِهَا.

وَفِي رِوَايَةِ ابْنِ عَبَّاسٍ ﷺ قَالَ: سَلُوا اللهَ بِبُطُونِ أَكُفِّكُمْ ولاَ تَسْأَلُوهُ بِظُهُورِهَا، وَإِذَا فَرَغْتُمْ فَامْسَحُوا بِهَا وُجُوهَكُمْ.

رَوَاهُ أَبُو دَاوُدَ

37 Mālik b. Yasār ﷺ said that Allah's Messenger ﷺ said: 'When you ask of Allah, ask Him with the palms of your hands (upward) and do not ask Him with their backs (upward).' And in the report of lbn 'Abbās ﷺ it says: 'Ask of Allah with the palms of your hands (upward) and do not ask Him with the backs (of your hands upward), and when you have finished, wipe your faces with them.'

Abū Dāwūd

<hr>

عَنْ أَبِي مُوسَى الأَشْعَرِيِّ ﷺ عَن النَّبِيِّ ﷺ أَنَّهُ كَانَ يَدْعُو: اللَّهُمَّ اغْفِرْ لِي خَطِيئَتِي وَجَهْلِي وَإِسْرَافِي فِي أَمْرِي ومَا أَنْتَ أَعْلَمُ بِهِ مِنِّي، اللَّهُمَّ اغْفِرْ لِي جِدِّي وَهَزْلِي وَخَطَئِي وَعَمْدِي وَكُلُّ ذَلِكَ عِنْدِي.

رَوَاهُ الْبُخَارِيُّ

38 Abū Mūsā al-Ash'arī ﷺ reported that the Prophet ﷺ used to supplicate: 'O Allah, forgive me my sins and my ignorance, my excesses in my matter and what you know better about than I myself. O Allah, forgive me the wrongs (I did) lightly and seriously, and my accidental and intentional transgressions, and all that is with me.'[1]

Bukhārī

---

[1] Arabic: *Allahumma-ghfirlī khaṭī'atī, wa jahlī wa isrāfī fī amrī wa mā anta a'lamu bihi minnī. Allahumma-ghfirlī hazlī wa jiddī wa khaṭa'ī wa 'amdī wa kullu dhālika 'indī.*

11

Fajr Prayer

عَنْ عَائِشَةَ رضي الله عنها أَنَّ رَسُولَ اللهِ ﷺ كَانَ يُصَلِّي رَكْعَتَيْنِ خَفِيفَتَيْنِ بَيْنَ النِّدَاءِ وَالإِقَامَةِ مِنْ صَلَاةِ الصُّبْحِ.

مُتَّفَقٌ عَلَيْهِ

39 ʿĀ'ishah رضي الله عنها said that Allah's Messenger ﷺ used to pray two short *rakʿas* between the call (of *adhān)* and the *iqāma*[1] of the *fajr* prayer.

Bukhārī, Muslim

عَنْ عَائِشَةَ رضي الله عنها قَالَتْ: كَانَ النَّبِيُّ ﷺ إِذَا صَلَّى رَكْعَتَيْ الفَجْرِ، فَإِنْ كُنْتُ مُسْتَيْقِظَةً حَدَثَنِي وَإِلَّا اضْطَجَعَ.

رَوَاهُ مُسْلِم

[1] The second call for prayer, immediately before the prayer begins. *Adhān* is the first call.

40 'Ā'ishah ﷺ said: 'The Prophet ﷺ, when he had prayed the two *rak'as* of the *fajr* prayer, used to talk with me, if I was awake. Otherwise, he would lie down.'

Muslim

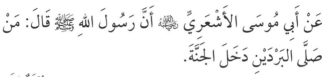

عَنْ أَبِي مُوسَى الأَشْعَرِيِّ ﷺ أَنَّ رَسُولَ اللهِ ﷺ قَالَ: مَنْ صَلَّى الْبَرْدَيْنِ دَخَلَ الْجَنَّةَ.

مُتَفَقٌ عَلَيْهِ

41 From Abū Mūsā al-Ash'arī ﷺ: Allah's Messenger ﷺ said: 'He who prays both morning and afternoon prayers will enter paradise.'

Bukhārī, Muslim

عَنْ عَائِشَةَ ﷺ قَالَتْ: كَانَ رَسُولُ اللهِ ﷺ يُصَلِّي الصُّبْحَ فَيَنْصَرِفُ نِسَاءُ الْمُؤْمِنِينَ مُتَلَفِّعَاتٍ بِمُرُوطِهِنَّ مَا يُعْرَفْنَ مِنَ الْغَلَسِ.

رَوَاهُ الْبُخَارِيُّ

42 'Ā'ishah ﷺ said: 'When Allah's Messenger ﷺ had performed the morning prayer, the women left, covered in their sheets, and they were not recognized because of the darkness.'

Bukhārī

12

Reading the Qur'ān
at Dawn

عَنْ أَبِي هُرَيْرَةَ ﷺ عَنِ النَّبِيِّ ﷺ فِي قَوْلِهِ تَعَالَى ﴿إِنَّ قُرْآنَ
الفَجْرِ كَانَ مَشْهُودًا﴾ قَالَ: تَشْهَدُهُ مَلائِكَةُ اللَّيْلِ وَمَلائِكَةُ
النَّهَارِ.

رَوَاهُ التِّرْمِذِيُّ

43

Abū Huraira ﷺ said that the Prophet ﷺ said about
Allah's word:[1] '(The recital of) the *Qur'ān* at dawn is
always witnessed – the angels of the night and the
angels of the day witness it.'

Tirmidhī

---

[1] *al-Isrā'* 17: 78

13

Forenoon Prayer

عَنْ مُعَاذِ بْنِ أَنَسِ الجُهَنِيّ ﷺ قَالَ: قَالَ رَسُولُ اللهِ ﷺ:
مَنْ قَعَدَ فِي مُصَلَّاهُ حِينَ يَنْصَرِفُ مِنْ صَلَاةِ الصُّبْحِ
حَتَّى يُسَبِّحَ رَكْعَتَيِ الضُّحَى لَا يَقُولُ إِلاَّ خَيْرًا غُفِرَ
لَهُ خَطَايَاهُ وَإِنْ كَانَتْ أَكْثَرَ مِنْ زَبَدِ البَحْرِ.
رَوَاهُ أَبُو دَاوُدَ

44 From Muʿādh b. Anas al-Juhanī ﷺ: Allah's Messenger ﷺ said: 'He who sits in the place where he has prayed, instead of leaving after the morning prayer, till he has praised (Allah with) two *rakʿas* of forenoon, saying only good, his sins are forgiven to him, even if they were more than the foam of the sea.'

Abū Dāwūd

14

Morning Toilet

عَنْ عَائِشَةَ رَضِيَ قَالَتْ: قَـالَ رَسُــولُ اللهِ ﷺ: عَشْرٌ مِنْ الْفِطْرَةِ: قَصُّ الشَّاربِ وَإِعْفَاءُ اللِّحْيَةِ وَالسِّوَاكُ واسْتِنْشَاقُ الْـمَـاءِ وَقَـصُّ الأَظْفَـارِ وَغَسْـلُ الْبَرَاجِمِ وَنَـتْفُ الإِبِطِ وَحَلْقُ الْعَانَةِ.

رَوَاهُ مُسْلِم

45 'A'ishah ﷺ said that Allah's Messenger ﷺ said: 'There are ten things related to man's nature: trimming the moustache, letting the beard (grow), brushing the teeth, using water to clean the nose, cutting the nails, washing clean the finger-joints, removing hair from under the armpits, shaving the pubes and using water (for cleansing after the call of nature).' The narrator said: 'I forgot the tenth, unless it was rinsing the mouth.'

Muslim

عَنْ أَنَسِ بْنِ مَالِكٍ ﴿ﷺ﴾ قَالَ: وَقَّتَ لَنَا رَسُولُ اللهِ ﷺ
أَرْبَعِينَ لَيْلَةً فِي قَصِّ الشَّارِبِ وَقَصِّ الأَظْفَارِ وَنَتْفِ الإِبِطِ
وَحَلْقِ الْعَانَةِ.

رَوَاهُ مُسْلِم

46 Anas b. Mālik ﷺ said: 'The Prophet ﷺ commanded us to trim the moustache, cut the nails, pluck (out hairs under) the armpits and shave the pubes every forty days.'

Muslim

عَنِ ابْنِ عُمَرَ ﴿ﷺ﴾ قَالَ: قَالَ رَسُولُ اللهِ ﷺ: أَحْفُوا الشَّوَارِبَ
وَأَعْفُوا اللِّحَى.

رَوَاهُ مُسْلِم

47 From Ibn 'Umar ﷺ: Allah's Messenger ﷺ said: 'Trim the moustache and let the beard (grow).'

Muslim

عَنْ عَطَاءِ بْنِ يَسَارٍ ﴿ﷺ﴾ قَالَ: كَانَ رَسُولُ اللهِ ﷺ فِي الْمَسْجِدِ
فَدَخَلَ رَجُلٌ ثَائِرُ الرَّأْسِ وَاللِّحْيَةِ فَأَشَارَ إِلَيْهِ رَسُولُ اللهِ

بِيَدِهِ ﷺ – كَأَنَّهُ يَأْمُرُهُ بِإِصْلَاحِ شَعْرِهِ ولِـحْيَتِهِ – فَفَعَلَ ثُمَّ رَجَعَ، فَقَالَ رَسُولُ الله ﷺ: أَلَيْسَ هَذَا خَيْرًا مِنْ أَنْ يَأْتِيَ أَحَدُكُمْ ثَائِرَ الرَّأْسِ كَأَنَّهُ شَيْطَانٌ.

رَوَاهُ مَالِكٌ

48 From 'Aṭā' b. Yasār ☙: Allah's Messenger ﷺ was in the mosque and a man entered with (the hair of his) head and beard untidy, and Allah's Messenger indicated with his hand that he should tidy his hair and beard. The man did so and then returned. Allah's Messenger said: 'Is this not better than that one of you comes and his hair is as though he were a devil?'

Mālik

عن عَمْرِو بْنِ شُعَيْبٍ عَنْ أَبِيهِ عَنْ جَدِّهِ ☙ قَالَ: قَالَ رَسُولُ الله ﷺ: لاتَنْتِفُوا الشِّيبَ فَإِنَّهُ نُورُ الْمُسْلِمِ. مَنْ شَابَ شِيبَةً فِي الإِسْلَامِ كَتَبَ اللهُ لَهُ بِهَا حَسَنَةً وَكَفَّرَ عَنْهُ بِهَا خَطِيئَةً وَرَفَعَهُ بِهَا دَرَجَةً.

رَوَاهُ أَبُو دَاوُدَ

49 From 'Amr b. Shu'aib, from his father, from his grandfather ﷺ: Allah's Messenger ﷺ said: 'Do not pluck grey hairs, for they are the light of the Muslim. (He) who grows a grey hair in Islam, Allah writes down for him a good deed for it, expiates a sin for it, and raises him a degree because of it.'

Abū Dāwūd

15

Clothing

عَنْ أُمِّ سَلَمَة ﷺ قَالَتْ: كَانَ أَحَبُّ الثِّيَابِ إِلَى رَسُولِ الله ﷺ القَمِيصَ.

رَوَاهُ أَبُو دَاوُدَ

50 Umm Salama ﷺ said: 'The (piece of) clothing best liked by Allah's Messenger ﷺ was the shirt.'

Tirmidhī, Abū Dāwūd

عَنْ أَبِي هُرَيْرَةَ ﷺ أَنَّ النَّبِيَّ ﷺ كَانَ إِذَا لَبِسَ قَمِيصًا بَدَأَ بِمَيَامِنِهِ.

رَوَاهُ التِّرْمِذِيُّ

51 Abū Huraira ﷺ said: 'Allah's Messenger ﷺ, when he put on a shirt, used to begin with the right side.'

Tirmidhī

عَنْ أَبِي هُرَيْرَةَ ﵁ أَنَّ رَسُولَ اللهِ ﷺ قَالَ: إِذَا انْتَعَلَ أَحَدُكُمْ فَلْيَبْدَأْ بِالْيَمِينِ وَإِذَا نَزَعَ فَلْيَبْدَأْ بِالشِّمَـالِ لِتَكُنِ الْيُمْنَى أَوَّلَـهُمَـا تُنْعَلُ وآخِرَهُمَا تُنْزَعُ.

مُتَّفَقٌ عَلَيْهِ

52 Abū Huraira ﵁ said that Allah's Messenger ﷺ said: 'When one of you puts on shoes, he should begin with the right one, and when he takes (his) shoes off, he should begin with the left one, so that the right one be the first of them to be put on and the last of them to be taken off.'

Bukhārī, Muslim

⁂

عَنْ مُعَاذِ بْنِ أَنَسٍ ﵁ أَنَّ النَّبِيَّ ﷺ قَالَ: مَنْ لَبِسَ ثَوْبًا فَقَالَ: الْحَمْدُ للهِ الَّذِي كَسَانِي هَذَا الثَّوْبَ وَرَزَقَنِيهِ مِنْ غَيْرِ حَوْلٍ مِنِّي وَلَا قُوَّةٍ، غُفِرَ لَهُ مَا تَقَدَّمَ مِنْ ذَنْبِهِ وَمَا تَأَخَّرَ.

رَوَاهُ أَبُو دَاوُدَ

53 From Muʿādh b. Anas ﵁: Allah's Messenger ﷺ said: 'He who puts on clothes and says: "Praise be to Allah, who clothed me with this, and who provided me with it, without any power or might of mine",[1] his past and future sins are forgiven to him.'

Abū Dāwūd

---

[1] Arabic: *Al-ḥamdu li-llāhi al-ladhī kasānī hādhā wa razaqanīhi min ghairi ḥawlin minnī wa lā quwwat.*

عَنْ عَمْرِو بْنِ شُعَيْبٍ عَنْ أَبِيهِ عَنْ جَدِّهِ ﷺ قَالَ: قَالَ
رَسُولُ اللهِ ﷺ: كُلُوا واشْرَبُوا وَتَصَدَّقُوا والْبَسُوا مَا لَمْ
يُخَالِطْ إِسْرَافٌ ولا مَخِيلَةٌ.

رَوَاهُ أَحْمَدُ والنَّسَائِي وابْنُ مَاجَه

54 From 'Amr b. Shu'aib, from his father, from his grandfather ﷺ: Allah's Messenger ﷺ said: 'Eat, drink, give *ṣadaqa* and wear (good) clothes as long as these things do not involve excess and arrogance.'

Aḥmad, Ibn Mājah

———— ❧ ————

عَنْ أَبِي أُمَامَةَ إِيَاسَ بْنِ ثَعْلَبَةَ ﷺ قَالَ: قَالَ رَسُولُ اللهِ ﷺ:
أَلا تَسْمَعُونِ! أَلا تَسْمَعُونِ! إِنَّ الْبَذَاذَةَ مِنَ الإِيمَانِ، إِنَّ
الْبَذَاذَةَ مِنَ الإِيمَانِ.

رَوَاهُ أَبُو دَاوُدَ

55 Abū Umāma Iyās b. Tha'laba ﷺ said that Allah's Messenger ﷺ said: 'Listen! Listen! Wearing old clothes is part of the faith, wearing old clothes is part of the faith!'

Abū Dāwūd

عَن عَمْرو بْنِ شُعَيْبٍ عَنْ أَبِيهِ عَنْ جَدِّهِ ﷺ قَـالَ: قَـالَ
رَسُولُ اللهِ ﷺ: إِنَّ اللهَ يُحِبُّ أَنْ يَرَى أَثَرَ نِعْمَتِهِ على عَبْدِهِ.
رَوَاهُ التِّرْمِذِيُّ

56 'Amr b. Shu'aib ⬥ reported from his father and his
grandfather ⬥, who said: Allah's Messenger ﷺ said:
'Allah likes to see the traces of His bounty on His
servant.'

Tirmidhī

⬥⬥⬥

عَنْ عَبْدِ اللهِ بْنِ عُمَرَ ﷺ أَنَّ رَسُولَ اللهِ ﷺ قَالَ: الَّذِي يَجُرُّ
ثَوْبَهُ خُيَلَاءَ لَا يَنْظُرُ اللهُ إِلَيْهِ يَوْمَ الْقِيَامَةِ. قَالَ أَبُو بَكْرٍ: يَا
رَسُولَ اللهِ! إِنَّ أَحَدَ شِقَّيْ إِزَارِي يَسْتَرْخِي، إِلَّا أَنْ أَتَعَاهَدَ
ذَلِكَ مِنْهُ. فَقَالَ النَّبِيُّ ﷺ: لَسْتَ مِمَّنْ يَصْنَعُهُ خُيَلَاءَ.
رَوَاهُ الْبُخَارِيُّ

57 'Abdullāh b. 'Umar ⬥ said that the Prophet ﷺ said:
'He who trails his dress in pride on the ground,
Allah will not look at him on the day of resurrection.'
Thereupon Abu Bakr said: 'O Allah's Messenger, my
izār[2] gets loose, until I tie it (again)'. And Allah's
Messenger said: 'You are not one of those who do
this out of pride.'

Bukhārī

---

[2] A type of loin cloth.

عَنْ ابْنِ عُمَرَ ﷺ قَالَ: قَالَ رَسُولُ اللهِ ﷺ: إِنَّمَا يَلْبَسُ
الْحَرِيرَ فِي الدُّنْيَا مَنْ لَا خَلاقَ لَهُ فِي الْآخِرَةِ.

رَوَاهُ الْبُخَارِيُّ

58 Ibn 'Umar said that Allah's Messenger said: 'Indeed
he who wears silk in this world (will) have no share
of it in the Hereafter.'

Bukhārī, Muslim

عَنْ أَبِي مُوسَى الْأَشْعَرِيِّ ﷺ أَنَّ النَّبِيَّ ﷺ قَالَ: أُحِلَّ
الذَّهَبُ والْحَرِيرُ لِلْإِنَاثِ مِنْ أُمَّتِي وَحُرِّمَ عَلَى ذُكُورِهَا.

رَوَاهُ أَحْمَدُ والنَّسَائِي والتِّرْمِذِيُّ

59 From Abū Mūsā al-Ash'arī ﷺ: The Prophet ﷺ said:
'Gold and silk are lawful to the women of my *ummah*
and prohibited to the men.'

Tirmidhī, Nasā'ī

عَنْ أَبِي هُرَيْرَةَ ﷺ قَالَ: لَعَنَ رَسُولُ اللهِ ﷺ الرَّجُلَ يَلْبَسُ
لِبْسَةَ الْمَرْأَةِ والْمَرْأَةُ تَلْبَسُ لِبْسَةَ الرَّجُلِ.

رَوَاهُ أَبُو دَاوُدَ

60 Abū Huraira ﷺ said: Allah's Messenger ﷺ cursed the man who put on women's clothes and the woman who put on men's clothes.

Abū Dāwūd

عَنْ عَائِشَةَ ﵍ أَنَّ أَسْمَاءَ بِنْتَ أَبِي بَكْرٍ ﵍ دَخَلَتْ عَلَى رَسُولِ
اللهِ ﷺ وعَلَيْهَا ثِيَابٌ رِقَاقٌ فَأَعْرَضَ عنْهَا رَسُولُ اللهِ ﷺ
وقَالَ: يَا أَسْمَاءُ! إِنَّ المَرْأَةَ إِذَا بَلَغَتِ المَحِيضَ لَنْ يَصْلُحَ أَنْ
يُرَى مِنْها إِلَّا هَذَا وَهَذَا، وأَشَارَ إِلَى وَجْهِهِ وَكَفَّيْهِ.
رَوَاهُ أَبُو دَاوُدَ

61 From 'Ā'ishah ﷺ: 'Once Asmā', the daughter of Abū Bakr ﷺ, came in to Allah's Messenger ﷺ with thin clothes on, so he turned away from her, saying: "O Asmā' When a woman reaches puberty, it is not right that any part of her (should) be seen but this and this," and he pointed to his face and his two hands.'

Abū Dāwūd

 16

Eating and Drinking

عَنْ سَلْمَانَ رضي الله عنه قَالَ: قَالَ رَسُولُ اللهِ ﷺ: بَرَكَةُ الطَّعَامِ الْوُضُوءُ قَبْلَهُ وبَعْدَهُ.

رَوَاهُ أَبُو دَاوُدَ

62 From Salmān ﷺ: Allah's Messenger ﷺ said: 'The blessing of food is (received by) washing (the hands) before and washing (the hands) after (taking) it.'

Tirmidhī, Abū Dāwūd

عَنْ عَائِشَةَ رضي الله عنها قَالَتْ: قَالَ رَسُولُ اللهِ ﷺ: إِذَا أَكَلَ أَحَدُكُمْ فَلْيَذْكُرِ اسْمَ اللهِ تَعَالَى، فَإِنْ نَسِيَ أَنْ يَذْكُرَ اسْمَ اللهِ تَعَالَى فِي أَوَّلِهِ فَلْيَقُلْ: بِسْمِ اللهِ فِي أَوَّلِهِ وآخِرِهِ.

رَوَاهُ أَبُو دَاوُدَ والتِّرْمِذِيُّ

63 'Ā'ishah ﷺ said that Allah's Messenger ﷺ said: 'When any one of you eats, he should invoke the name of Allah the Exalted. If he forgets to invoke the name of Allah the Exalted at the beginning, he should say (when he does remember): "ln the name of Allah, in its beginning and its end."'[1]

Abū Dāwūd, Tirmidhī

عَنْ أَبِي سَعِيدٍ الْخُدْرِيِّ ﴿ أَنَّ النَّبِيَّ ﷺ كَانَ إِذَا فَرَغَ مِنْ طَعَامِهِ قَالَ: الْـحَمْـدُ للهِ الذِي أَطْـعَـمَـنَا وسَـقَانَا وَجَعَلَنَا مُسْلِمِينَ.

رَوَاهُ التِّرْمِذِيُّ وَأَبُو دَاوُدَ وابْنُ مَاجَه

64 Abū Saʿīd al-Khudrī ﷺ said that Allah's Messenger ﷺ, when he finished his meal, used to say: 'Praise be to Allah, Who gave us to eat and to drink and made us Muslims.'[2]

Tirmidhī, Abū Dāwūd, lbn Mājah

---

[1] Arabc: *Bismi-llāhi fī awwalihi wa ākhirih.*
[2] Arabic: *Al-ḥamdu li-llāhi al-ladhī aṭʿamanā wa saqānā wa jaʿalanā muslimīn.*

عَنْ عُمَرَ بْنِ أَبِي سَلَمَةَ ﷺ قَالَ: كُنْتُ غُلاَمًا فِي حِجْرِ النَّبِيِّ ﷺ وَكَانَتْ يَدِي تَطِيشُ فِي الصَّحْفَةِ، فَقَالَ النَّبِيُّ ﷺ: يَا غُلاَمُ سَمِّ اللهَ وَكُلْ بِيَمِينِكَ وَكُلْ مِمَّا يَلِيكَ.

رَوَاهُ مُسْلِم

65 'Umar b. Abū Salama ﷺ said: 'I was under the care of Allah's Messenger ﷺ and my hand used to pick at random in the dish, so Allah's Messenger said to me: "Invoke the name of Allah and eat with your right (hand) and eat what is near you."'

Muslim

عَنْ أَبِي هُرَيْرَةَ ﷺ قَالَ: مَا عَابَ رَسُولُ اللهِ ﷺ طَعَامًا قَطُّ، كَانَ إِذَا اشْتَهَى شَيْئًا أَكَلَهُ وَإِنْ كَرِهَهُ تَرَكَهُ.

رَوَاهُ مُسْلِم

66 From Abū Huraira ﷺ: Allah's Messenger ﷺ never found fault with food. If he liked something, he ate it, but if he disliked it, he (just) abstained from it.

Muslim

عَنْ كَعْبِ بْنِ مَالِكٍ ﷺ قَالَ : كَانَ رَسُولُ اللهِ ﷺ يَأْكُلُ
بِثَلاثَةِ أَصَابِعَ وَيَلْعَقُ يَدَهُ قَبْلَ أَنْ يَمْسَحَهَا.

رَوَاهُ مُسْلِم

67 From Ka'b b. Mālik ﷺ: Allah's Messenger ﷺ used to eat with three fingers, and he licked his hand before he wiped it.

Muslim

عَنْ أَنَسِ بْنِ مَالِكٍ ﷺ قَالَ : كَانَ رَسُولُ اللهِ ﷺ إِذَا أَكَلَ
طَعَامًا لَعِقَ أَصَابِعَهُ الثَّلاثَ. قَالَ: وَقَالَ: إِذَا سَقَطَتْ لُقْمَةُ
أَحَدِكُمْ فَلْيُمِطْ عَنْهَا الأَذَى وَلْيَأْكُلْهَا ولَايَدَعْهَا للشَّيْطَانِ.
وَأَمَرَنَا أَنْ نَسْلُتَ القَصْعَةَ، وقَالَ: إِنَّكُمْ لاَتَدْرُونَ فِي أَيِّ
طَعَامِكُمُ البَرَكَةُ.

رَوَاهُ مُسْلِم

68 From Anas b. Mālik ﷺ: When Allah's Messenger ﷺ ate food, he used to lick his three fingers and he said: 'When one of you drops a morsel, he should remove the dirt from it and eat it, and should not leave it for the *Shaiṭān*.' And he ordered us to wipe the bowl. He said: 'You do not know in which (part) of your food is the *baraka*.'[3]

Muslim

---

[3] The blessings from Allah.

عَنْ جَبَلَةَ بْنُ سُحَيْمٍ ﷺ قَالَ: أَصَابَنَا عَامُ سَنَةٍ مَعَ ابْنِ
الزُّبَيْرِ فَرَزَقْنَا تَمْرًا فَكَانَ عَبْدُ اللهِ بْنُ عُمَرَ ﷺ يَمُرُّ بِنَا وَنَحْنُ
نَأْكُلُ فَيَقُولُ: لَا تُقَارِنُوا فَإِنَّ النَّبِيَّ ﷺ نَهَى عَنِ القِرَانِ، ثُمَّ
يَقُولُ: إِلَّا أَنْ يَسْتَأْذِنَ الرَّجُلُ أَخَاهُ.

مُتَّفَقٌ عَلَيْهِ

69 Jabala b. Suḥaim ﷺ said: 'A year of famine befell us
while we were with Ibn Zubair. We lived on dates,
and when 'Abdullāh b. 'Umar ﷺ passed by us while
we were eating, he said: "Do not take two at a time,
for the Prophet ﷺ has prohibited the taking of two
at a time." Then he added: "Except when a man has
permitted his brother to do so."'

Bukhārī, Muslim

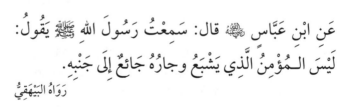

عَنِ ابْنِ عَبَّاسٍ ﷺ قَالَ: سَمِعْتُ رَسُولَ اللهِ ﷺ يَقُولُ:
لَيْسَ الْـمُؤْمِنُ الَّذِي يَشْبَعُ وجَارُهُ جَائِعٌ إِلَى جَنْبِهِ.

رَوَاهُ البَيْهَقِيُّ

70 From Ibn 'Abbās ﷺ: I heard Allah's Messenger ﷺ
say: 'The believer is not he who eats his fill while his
neighbour at his side is hungry.'

Baihaqī

عَنْ أَبِي هُرَيْرَةَ ﷺ قَالَ: قَالَ رَسُولُ الله ﷺ: طَعَامُ الِاثْنَيْنِ كَافِي الثَّلَاثَةِ وطَعَامُ الثَّلَاثَةِ كَافِي الأَرْبَعَةِ.

رَوَاهُ مُسْلِم

71 From Abū Huraira ﷺ: Allah's Messenger ﷺ said: 'Food for two is sufficient for three, and food for three is sufficient for four.'

Muslim

عَنْ عُمَرَ بْنِ الخَطَّابِ ﷺ قَالَ: قَالَ رَسُولَ الله ﷺ: كُلُوا جَمِيعًا وَلَا تَفَرَّقُوا، فَإِنَّ البَرَكَةَ فِي الجَمَاعَةِ.

رَوَاهُ ابْنُ مَاجَه

72 From 'Umar b. al-Khaṭṭāb ﷺ: Allah's Messenger ﷺ said: 'Eat together, and do not separate, for the blessing is in the company.'

Ibn Mājah

عَنْ جَعْفَرِ بْنِ مُحَمَّدٍ عَنْ أَبِيهِ ﷺ قَالَ: كَانَ رَسُولُ الله ﷺ إِذَا أَكَلَ مَعَ قَوْمٍ كَانَ آخِرَهُمْ أَكْلًا.

رَوَاهُ البَيْهَقِيُّ

73 From Ja'far b. Muḥammad, from his father ﷺ: Allah's Messenger ﷺ, when he ate with other people, was usually the last to finish eating.

Baihaqī

عَنْ أَبِي كَرِيمَةَ المِقْدَامِ بْنِ مَعْدِي كَرِبٍ رِضِيَ اللهُ عَنْهُ قَالَ: سَمِعْتُ
رَسُولَ اللهِ ﷺ يَقُولُ: مَا مَلَأَ آدَمِيٌّ وِعَاءً شَرًّا مِنْ بَطْنٍ،
بِحَسْبِ ابْنِ آدَمَ أُكُلَاتٌ يُقِمْنَ صُلْبَهُ، فَإِنْ كَانَ لَا مَحَالَةَ
فَثُلُثٌ لِطَعَامِهِ وَثُلُثٌ لِشَرَابِهِ وَثُلُثٌ لِنَفَسِهِ.

رَوَاهُ التِّرْمِذِيُّ

74 Abū Karīma al-Miqdām b. Ma'dī Karib ﷺ said that he heard Allah's Messenger ﷺ say: 'No man fills a vessel which is worse than his stomach. Sufficient for the son of Adam are a few mouthfuls to keep his back upright, but if it has to be more, then let one third (of the stomach) be for his food, one third for his drink and one third (be left) for his breathing.'

Tirmidhī

عَنْ أَبِي قَتَادَةَ عَنْ أَبِيهِ رِضِيَ اللهُ عَنْهُ أَنَّ النَّبِيَّ ﷺ نَهَى أَنْ يُتَنَفَّسَ
فِي الإِنَاءِ.

رَوَاهُ مُسْلِم

75 From Abū Qatāda, from his father ﷺ: Allah's Messenger ﷺ forbade breathing into a vessel.

Muslim

عَنْ أَنَسٍ ﷺ قَالَ كَانَ رَسُولُ الله ﷺ يَتَنَفَّسُ في الشَّرَابِ ثَلَاثًا وَيَقُولُ: إِنَّهُ أَرْوَى وَأَبْرَأُ وَأَمْرَأُ. قَالَ أَنَسٌ: فَأَنَا أَتَنَفَّسُ في الشَّرَابِ ثَلَاثًا.

رَوَاهُ مُسْلِم

76 Anas ﷺ said: Allah's Messenger ﷺ used to take three breaths while drinking, and he said: 'It is more thirst-quenching, and more healthy, and more wholesome.' Anas said: 'So I also take three breaths while drinking.'

Muslim

عَنْ أَنَسِ بْنِ مَالِكٍ ﷺ قَالَ : قَالَ رَسُولُ الله ﷺ: إِنَّ اللهَ لَيَرْضَى عَنِ الْعَبْدِ يَأْكُلُ الأَكْلَةَ فَيَحْمَدُهُ عَلَيْهَا أَوْ يَشْرَبُ فَيَحْمَدُهُ عَلَيْهَا .

رَوَاهُ مُسْلِم

77 Anas b. Mālik ☙ said that Allah's Messenger ﷺ said: 'Allah is indeed pleased with His servant who, when he eats a morsel, praises Him for it, or drinks a sip and then praises Him for it.'

Muslim

عَنْ عَائِشَةَ ﵂ عَنِ النَّبِيِّ ﷺ أَنَّهُ قَالَ: إِذَا وُضِعَ الْعَشَاءُ
وَأُقِيمَتِ الصَّلَاةُ فَابْدَءُوا بِالْعَشَاءِ.

رَوَاهُ الْبُخَارِيُّ

78 From 'Ā'ishah ﵂: The Prophet ﷺ said: 'If dinner is served and *iqāma* for prayer is (also) said, then take the dinner first.'

Bukhārī

عَنْ حُذَيْفَةَ ﵁ قَالَ: إِنِّي سَمِعْتُ رَسُولَ اللهِ ﷺ يَقُولُ:
لَا تَلْبَسُوا الْحَرِيرَ وَلَا الدِّيبَاجَ وَلَا تَشْرَبُوا فِي آنِيَةِ الذَّهَبِ
وَالْفِضَّةِ، هُوَ لَهُمْ فِي الدُّنْيَا وَهُوَ لَكُمْ فِي الآخِرَةِ.

رَوَاهُ مُسْلِم

79 Ḥudhaifa ﷺ said that he heard Allah's Messenger ﷺ
say: 'Do not wear silk and brocade, and do not drink
from vessels of gold or silver, and do not eat from
plates made thereof, for these are for them[4] in this
world.'

Muslim

---

[4] Nawawī in his commentary on the *ṣaḥīḥ* of Muslim says
this refers to the unbelievers.

❈ 17 ❈

Leaving the House

عَنْ أَنَس بْنِ مَالِكٍ رَضِيَ اللهُ عَنْهُ أَنَّ النَّبِيَّ ﷺ قَالَ: إِذَا خَرَجَ الرَّجُلُ مِنْ بَيْتِهِ فَقَالَ بِسْمِ اللهِ تَوَكَّلْتُ عَلَى اللهِ لَا حَوْلَ وَلَا قُوَّةَ إِلَّا بِاللهِ، يُقَالُ لَهُ حِينَئِذٍ: هُدِيتَ وَكُفِيتَ وَوُقِيتَ، فَتَتَنَحَّى لَهُ الشَّيَاطِينُ. فَيَقُولُ لَهُ شَيْطَانٌ آخَرُ كَيْفَ لَكَ بِرَجُلٍ قَدْ هُدِيَ وَكُفِيَ وَوُقِيَ.

رَوَاهُ أَبُو دَاوُدَ

80 Anas b. Mālik ؓ said that Allah's Messenger ﷺ said: 'When a man leaves his house, saying: "In the name of Allah, I trust in Allah, there is no might and power but in Allah,"[1] it is said to him at that time: "You are guided, you are taken care of, you are protected." Then the *Shaiṭān* turns away from him, and another *Shaiṭān* says: "How can a man be for you, who is already guided, cared for and protected?"'

Abū Dāwūd

---

[1] Arabic: *Bismi-llāh. Tawakkaltu ʿalā llāh wa lā ḥawla wa lā quwwata illā bi-llāh.*

18

Saying *Salām*

عَنْ عَبْدِ اللهِ بْنِ عَمْرٍو ﷺ أَنَّ رَجُلًا سَأَلَ رَسُولَ اللهِ ﷺ:
أَيُّ الإِسْلَامِ خَيْرٌ؟ قَالَ: تُطْعِمِ الطَّعَامَ وتُقْرِأُ السَّلَامَ عَلَى
مَنْ عَرَفْتَ وَمَنْ لَمْ تَعْرِفْ.
مُتَّفَقٌ عَلَيْه

81 From 'Abdūllāh b. 'Amr ﷺ: A man asked Allah's
Messenger ﷺ: 'Which part of lslam is best?' He said:
'To provide food and to say *salām*[1] to those you know
and to those you do not know.'

Bukhārī, Muslim

---

[1] The Muslim greeting is: Peace be upon you, '*as-salāmu
'alaikum*' and the response is: And upon you be peace, '*wa-
'alaikumu-salām*'.

عَنْ أَبِي أُمَامَةَ الْبَاهِلِيِّ ﷺ قَالَ: قَالَ رَسُـولُ اللهِ ﷺ: إِنَّ أَوْلَى النَّاسِ بِاللهِ مَنْ بَدَأَ بِالسَّلام.

رَوَاهُ أَحْمَدُ والتِّرْمِذِيُّ وَأَبُو دَاوُدَ

82 Abū Umāma al-Bāhilī said that Allah's Messenger
ﷺ said: 'Indeed the nearest of people to Allah are
they who begin with saying *salām*.'

Tirmidhī, Abū Dāwūd, Aḥmad

عَنْ أَبِي هُرَيْرَةَ ﷺ عَنِ النَّبِيِّ ﷺ أَنَّهُ قَالَ: إِذَا لَقِيَ أَحَدُكُمْ أَخَاهُ فَلْيُسَلِّمْ عَلَيْهِ، فَإِنْ حَالَتْ بَيْنَهُمَا شَجَرَةٌ أَوْ جِدَارٌ وَلَقِيَهُ فَلْيُسَلِّمْ عَلَيْهِ.

رَوَاهُ أَبُو دَاوُد

83 Abū Huraira said that Allah's Messenger ﷺ said:
'When one of you meets his brother, he should say
salām to him. If a tree or a wall or a rock comes in
between them, and then they meet again, he should
(again) say *salām* to him.'

Abū Dāwūd

عَنْ أَبِي هُرَيْرَةَ ﷺ قَالَ: قَالَ رَسُولُ اللهِ ﷺ: يُسَلِّمُ الصَّغِيرُ عَلَى الْكَبِيرِ وَالْمَارُّ عَلَى الْقَاعِدِ وَالْقَلِيلُ عَلَى الْكَثِيرِ .

رَوَاهُ الْبُخَارِيُّ

84 Abū Huraira ﷺ said that Allah's Messenger ﷺ said: 'The young should say *salām* to the old, the passer-by to the one sitting, and the small (group) to the large one.'

Bukhārī

عَنْ جَابِرِ بْنِ عَبْدِ اللهِ ﷺ أَنَّ النَّبِيَّ ﷺ مَرَّ عَلَى نِسْوَةٍ فَسَلَّمَ عَلَيْهِنَّ.

رَوَاهُ أَحْمَد

85 From Jābir b. 'Abdullāh ﷺ: The Prophet ﷺ passed by (some) women and said *salām* to them.

Aḥmad

عَنْ أَنَسٍ ﷺ أَنَّهُ مَرَّ عَلَى صِبْيَانٍ فَسَلَّمَ عَلَيْهِمْ وَقَالَ: كَانَ النَّبِيُّ ﷺ يَفْعَلُهُ.

مُتَفَقٌ عَلَيْهِ

86 From Anas ﷺ, who passed some children and said *salām* to them and said: 'The Prophet ﷺ used to do this.'

Bukhārī, Muslim

عَنْ أَبِي أُمَامَةَ ﷺ أَنَّ رَسُولَ اللهِ ﷺ قَالَ: تَمَامُ تَحِيَّاتِكُمْ بَيْنَكُمُ الْمُصَافَحَةُ.

رَوَاهُ أَحْمَد والترمذيُّ

87 From Abū Umāma ﷺ: Allah's Messenger ﷺ said: 'The best (way) of greeting is shaking hands.'

Aḥmad, Tirmidhī

19

Sneezing and Yawning

عَنْ أَبِي سَعِيدٍ الْخُدْرِيِّ ﴿ﷺ﴾ أَنَّ رَسُولَ اللهِ ﴿ﷺ﴾ قَالَ: إِذَا تَثَاءَبَ أَحَدُكُمْ فَلْيُمْسِكْ بِيَدِهِ عَلَى فَمِهِ فَإِنَّ الشَّيْطَانَ يَدْخُلُ.

رَوَاهُ مُسْلِم

88 From Abū Saʿīd al-Khudrī ﷺ: Allah's Messenger ﷺ said: 'When one of you yawns, he should hold his hand over his mouth, for the *Shaiṭān* enters (through the open mouth).'

Muslim

عَنْ أَبِي هُرَيْرَةَ ﴿ﷺ﴾ قَالَ: كَانَ رَسُولُ اللهِ ﴿ﷺ﴾ إِذَا عَطَسَ وَضَعَ يَدَهُ أَوْ ثَوْبَهُ عَلَى وَجْهِهِ وخَفَضَ – أَوْ غَضَّ – بِهَا صَوْتَهُ.

رَوَاهُ أَبُو دَاوُد والترْمِذِيُّ

89 From Abū Huraira ﷺ: Allah's Messenger ﷺ, when he sneezed, used to hold his hand or a cloth over his mouth and soften or diminish its sound with it.

Abū Dāwūd, Tirmidhī

عَنْ أَبِي هُرَيْرَةَ ﷺ قَـالَ: قَالَ رَسُـولَ الله ﷺ: إِذَا عَطَسَ أَحَدُكُمْ فَلْيَقُلْ: الحَمْدُ لله، وَلْيَقُلْ لَهُ أَخُوهُ – أَوْ صَاحِبُهُ –: يَرْحَمُكَ الله. فَإِذَا قَالَ لَهُ: يَرْحَمُكَ الله، فَلْيَقُلْ: يَهْدِيكُمُ الله وَيُصْلِحْ بَالَكُمْ.

رَوَاهُ البُخَارِيُّ

90 From Abū Huraira ﷺ: Allah's Messenger ﷺ said: 'When one of you sneezes, he should say: "Praise be to Allah,"[1] and his brother should say: "Allah have mercy on you."[2] When he says: "Allah have mercy on you," he should reply: "Allah guide you and better your affairs."'[3]

Bukhārī

---

[1] Arabic: *Al-ḥamdu li-llāh.*
[2] Arabic: *Yarḥamuka llāh.*
[3] Arabic: *Yahdīkumu Ilāh wa yuṣliḥ bālakum.*

20

Earning a Livelihood

عَنْ عَبْدِ اللهِ بْنِ مَسْعُودٍ ﷺ قَالَ: قَالَ رَسُـولُ اللهِ ﷺ:
كَسْبُ الْحَلَالِ فَرِيضَةٌ بَعْدَ الْفَرِيضَةِ.

رَوَاهُ البَيْهَقِيُّ

91 From 'Abdullāh b. Mas'ūd ﷺ: Allah's Messenger ﷺ
said: 'To try to earn a lawful livelihood is (also) an
obligation like the other obligations (in Islam).'

Baihaqī

عَنْ أَبِي عَبْدِ اللهِ، وَيُقَالُ لَهُ أَبُو عَبْدِ الرَّحْمَنِ ثَوْبَانَ ﷺ، قَالَ:
قَالَ رَسُولُ اللهِ ﷺ: أَفْضَلُ دِينَارٍ دِينَارٌ يُنْفِقُهُ الرَّجُلُ عَلَى
عِيَالِهِ وَدِينَارٌ يُنْفِقُهُ عَلَى دَابَّتِهِ فِي سَبِيلِ اللهِ وَدِينَارٌ يُنْفِقُهُ عَلَى
أَصْحَابِهِ فِي سَبِيلِ اللهِ.

رَوَاهُ مُسْلِم

92 Abū 'Abdullāh, who was called 'Abd al-Raḥmān Thawbān ﷺ said: Allah's Messenger ﷺ said: 'The best *dīnār*[1] a man spends is the *dīnār* he spends on his family, and the *dīnār* he spends on his riding beast in the path of Allah, and the *dīnār* he spends on his companions in the path of Allah.'

Muslim

عَنِ الْـمِقْدَامِ ﷺ عَنْ رَسُولِ اللهِ ﷺ قَالَ: مَا أَكَلَ أَحَدٌ
طَعَامًا قَطُّ خَيْرًا مِنْ أَنْ يَأْكُلَ مِنْ عَمَلِ يَدِهِ ...
رَوَاهُ الْبُخَارِيُّ

93 From al-Miqdam ﷺ: Allah's Messenger ﷺ said: 'No one has ever eaten better food than what he eats from the work done by his hands...'

Bukhārī

عَنْ عَائِشَةَ ﷺ قَالَتْ: كَانَ أَصْحَابُ رَسُولِ اللهِ ﷺ عُمَّالَ
أَنْفُسِهِمْ، وَكَانَ يَكُونُ لَهُمْ أَرْوَاحٌ فَقِيلَ لَهُمْ لَوِ اغْتَسَلْتُمْ.
رَوَاهُ الْبُخَارِيُّ

---

[1] The *Dīnār* was the unit of currency in the Prophet's time, but in this case it means 'coin' or 'money'

94 'Ā'ishah ﷺ said: 'The Companions of Allah's Messenger ﷺ used to be their own labourers, and the smell (of sweat) used to be on them, so it was said to them: "You should (regularly) bath."'

Bukhārī

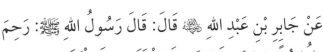

عَنْ جَابِرِ بْنِ عَبْدِ الله ﷺ قَالَ: قَالَ رَسُولُ الله ﷺ: رَحِمَ اللهُ رَجُلًا سَمْحًا إِذَا بَاعَ وَإِذَا اشْتَرَى وَإِذَا اقْتَضَى.
رَوَاهُ الْبُخَارِيُّ

95 From Jābir b. 'Abdullāh ﷺ: Allah's Messenger ﷺ said: 'May Allah have mercy on a man who is kind when he buys, when he sells and when he makes a demand.'

Bukhārī

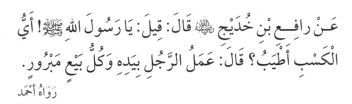

عَـنْ رافِـعِ بْنِ خُدَيْجٍ ﷺ قَالَ: قِيلَ: يَا رَسُولَ الله ﷺ! أَيُّ الْكَسْبِ أَطْيَبُ؟ قَالَ: عَمَلُ الرَّجُلِ بِيَدِهِ وَكُلُّ بَيْعٍ مَبْرُورٍ.
رَوَاهُ أَحْمَد

96 Rāfi' b. Khudaij ﷺ said that someone asked: 'O Allah's Messenger ﷺ, which gain is best?' He said: 'A man's work by his hand, and every honest business.'

Aḥmad

عَنْ عَبْدِ اللهِ بْنِ عُمَرَ ﷺ قَالَ: قَالَ رَسُولُ اللهِ ﷺ: أَعْطُوا
الْأَجِيرَ أَجْرَهُ قَبْلَ أَنْ يَجِفَّ عَرَقُهُ.

رَوَاهُ ابْنُ مَاجَه

97 'Abdullāh b. 'Umar ☙ said: Allah's Messenger ﷺ
said: 'Give the labourer his wages before his sweat
dries.'

Ibn Mājah

━━━━━◦◦◦◦◦━━━━━

عَنْ أَبِي هُرَيْرَةَ ﷺ عَنِ النَّبِيِّ ﷺ أَنَّهُ قَالَ: يَأْتِي عَلَى النَّاسِ
زَمَانٌ لَا يُبَالِي الْمَرْءُ مَا أَخَذَ مِنْهُ أَمِنَ الْحَلَالِ أَمْ مِنَ الْحَرَامِ.

رَوَاهُ الْبُخَارِيُّ

98 Abū Huraira ☙ said that Allah's Messenger ﷺ said:
'A time will come upon mankind when a man will not
care whether what he takes is lawful or unlawful.'

Bukhārī

━━━━━◦◦◦◦◦━━━━━

عَنْ أَبِي أُمَامَةَ إِيَاسَ بْنِ ثَعْلَبَةَ الْـحَـارِثِيِّ ﷺ أَنَّ رَسُولَ
اللهِ ﷺ قَالَ: مَنِ اقْتَطَعَ حَقَّ امْرِئٍ مُسْلِمٍ بِيَمِينِهِ فَقَدْ أَوْجَبَ
اللهُ لَهُ النَّارَ وَحَرَّمَ عَلَيْهِ الْجَنَّةَ. فَقَالَ رَجُلٌ: وَإِنْ كَانَ شَيْئًا

يَسِيرًا يَا رَسُولَ اللهِ! قَالَ: وَإِنْ قَضِيبًا مِنْ أَرَاكٍ، وَإِنْ قَضِيبًا مِنْ أَرَاكٍ، وَإِنْ قَضِيبًا مِنْ أَرَاكٍ.

رَوَاهُ مُسْلِم

99 Abū Umāma b. Iyās b. Tha 'laba al-Ḥārithī ﷺ said that Allah's Messenger ﷺ said: 'He who usurps the right in a Muslim's affair by false oath, Allah has laid the fire on him and has prevented him from (entering) paradise.' Thereupon a man said: 'And if it was only something insignificant, O Allah's Messenger?' He said: 'Even if it was a twig of the *arak*[2] tree.' He repeated it three times.

Muslim

⸺⸺⸺⊷⊶⸺⸺⸺

عَنْ عَائِشَةَ رَضِيَ اللهُ عَنْهَا أَنَّ رَسُولَ اللهِ ﷺ قَالَ: مَنْ ظَلَمَ قَيْدَ شِبْرٍ مِنَ الْأَرْضِ طُوِّقَهُ مِنْ سَبْعِ أَرَضِينَ يَوْمَ الْقِيَامَةِ.

مُتَّفَقٌ عَلَيْهِ

100 'Ā'ishah ﷺ said that Allah's Messenger ﷺ said: 'He who unjustly takes land measuring but a hand-span will have sevenfold the measure of that land hanged around his neck.'

Bukhārī, Muslim

---

[2] The name of a tree found in Arabia.

21

General Conduct

عَنْ أَبِي هُرَيْرَةَ ﷺ قَالَ: سَمِعْتُ رَسُولَ الله ﷺ يَقُولُ: وَالله
إِنِّي لَأَسْتَغْفِرُ الله وَأَتُوبُ إِلَيْهِ فِي الْيَوْمِ أَكْثَرَ مِنْ سَبْعِينَ مَرَّةً.
رَوَاهُ الْبُخَارِيُّ

101 Abū Huraira ﷺ said: 'I heard Allah's Messenger ﷺ
say: "By Allah, I ask Allah's forgiveness and turn to
Him in repentance more than seventy times a day."'
Bukhārī

عَنْ عَبْدِ الله بْنِ عَمْرٍو ﷺ قَالَ: قَالَ رَسُولُ الله ﷺ: أَرْبَعٌ
مَنْ كُنَّ فِيهِ كَانَ مُنَافِقًا خَالِصًا: إِذَا حَدَّثَ كَذَبَ وَإِذَا وَعَدَ
أَخْلَفَ وَإِذَا عَاهَدَ غَدَرَ وَإِذَا خَاصَمَ فَجَرَ. فَمَنْ كَانَتْ فِيهِ
خَصْلَةٌ مِنْهُنَّ كَانَتْ فِيهِ خَصْلَةٌ مِنَ النِّفَاقِ حَتَّى يَدَعَهَا .
رَوَاهُ الْبُخَارِيُّ

102 'Abdullāh b. 'Amr reported that the Prophet said: 'There are four traits; he who has all of them is a certain hypocrite and he who has one of them has some hypocrisy, until he gets rid of it: when being given a trust, he betrays; when he speaks, he lies; when he promises (something), he breaks it; and when he quarrels, he commits excesses.'

Bukharī

عَنْ عَبْدِ اللهِ بْنِ مَسْعُودٍ ﷺ قَالَ: قَالَ رَسُولُ اللهِ ﷺ:
سِبَابُ الْـمُسْلِمِ فُسُوقٌ وَقِتَالُهُ كُفْرٌ.

مُتَّفَقٌ عَلَيْهِ

103 'Abdullāh b. Mas'ūd said that Allah's Messenger said: 'Abusing a Muslim is sinful and fighting with, him is (tantamount to) *kufr*.'[1]

Bukhārī, Muslim

عَنْ عَبْدِ اللهِ بْنِ عَمْرٍو ﷺ قَالَ: قَالَ رَسُــولُ اللهِ ﷺ:
الْـمُسْلِمُ مَنْ سَلِمَ الْـمُسْلِمُونَ مِنْ لِسَانِهِ وَيَدِهِ وَالْـمُهَاجِرُ
مِنْ هَجَرَ مَا نَهَى اللهُ عَنْهُ.

مُتَّفَقٌ عَلَيْهِ

---

[1] Rejection of faith.

104 'Abdullāh b. 'Amr ﷺ said that Allah's Messenger ﷺ said: 'The Muslim is he from whose tongue and hand the Muslims are safe, and the *muhājir*[2] is he who gives up what Allah has prohibited for him.'

Bukhārī, Muslim

عَنْ أَبِي هُرَيْرَةَ ﵁ عَنِ النَّبِيِّ ﷺ أَنَّهُ قَالَ: إِيَّاكُمْ وَالْحَسَدَ
فَإِنَّ الْحَسَدَ يَأْكُلُ الْحَسَنَاتِ كَمَا تَأْكُلُ النَّارُ الْحَطَبَ.

رَوَاهُ أَبُو دَاوُد

105 Abū Huraira ﷺ reported that the Prophet ﷺ said: 'Beware of envy, for envy devours good (deeds) like fire devours firewood.'

Abū Dāwūd

عَنْ أَبِي هُرَيْرَةَ ﵁ أَنَّ رَسُولَ اللهِ ﷺ قَالَ: إِيَّاكُمْ وَالظَّنَّ
فَإِنَّ الظَّنَّ أَكْذَبُ الْحَدِيثِ وَلَا تَحَسَّسُوا وَلَا تَجَسَّسُوا
وَلَا تَنَافَسُوا وَلَا تَحَاسَدُوا وَلَا تَبَاغَضُوا وَلَا تَدَابَرُوا
وَكُونُوا عِبَادَ اللهِ إِخْوَانًا كَمَا أَمَرَكُمْ. الْمُسْلِمُ أَخُ

---

[2] One who makes a *Hijra* or emigration.

الـمُسْلِم، لَا يَظْلِمُهُ وَلَا يَخْذُلُهُ وَلَا يَحْقِرُهُ. التَّقْوَى هَاهُنَا، التَّقْوَى هَاهُنَا – وَيُشِيرُ إِلَى صَدْرِهِ – بِحَسَبِ امْرِئٍ مِنَ الشَّرِ أَنْ يَحْقِرَ أَخَاهُ الْمُسْلِمَ. كُلُّ الْمُسْلِم عَلَى الْمُسْلِم حَرَامٌ دَمُهُ وَعِرْضُهُ وَمَالُهُ. إِنَّ اللهَ لَا يَنْظُرُ إِلَى أَجْسَادِكُمْ وَلَا إِلَى صُوَرِكُمْ وَأَعْمَالِكُمْ وَلَكِنْ يَنْظُرُ إِلَى قُلُوبِكُمْ.

مُتَّفَقٌ عَلَيْهِ

106 Abū Huraira ⁣ reported that Allah's Messenger ﷺ said: 'Beware of suspicion, for suspicion is the greatest falsehood. Do not try to find fault with each other, do not spy on one another, do not vie with one another, do not envy one another, do not be angry with one another, do not turn away from one another, and be servants of Allah, brothers to one another, as you have been enjoined. A Muslim is the brother of a Muslim – he does him no wrong, nor does he let him down; nor does he despise him. Fear of God is here, fear of God is here,' – and he pointed to his chest. 'It is evil enough that a Muslim should look down on his brother. For every Muslim is sacred to another – his blood, his honour and his property. Allah does not look at your bodies or your forms, or your deeds, but He looks at your hearts.'

Bukhārī, Muslim

عَنْ أَبِي سَعِيدٍ الخُدْرِيِّ ﷺ عَنِ النَّبِيِّ ﷺ قَالَ: إِيَّاكُمْ
وَالْجُلُوسَ فِي الطُّرُقَاتِ. قَالُوا: يا رَسُولَ اللهِ! مَا لَنَا مِنْ
مَجَالِسِنَا بُدٌّ، نَتَحَدَّثُ فِيهَا. فَقَالَ رَسُولُ اللهِ ﷺ: فَإِذَا أَبَيْتُمْ
إِلَّا الْمَجْلِسَ فَأَعْطُوا الطَّرِيقَ حَقَّهُ. قَالُوا: وَمَا حَقُّ الطَّرِيقِ
يَا رَسُولَ اللهِ؟ قَالَ: غَضُّ البَصَرِ وَكَفُّ الأَذَى وَرَدُّ السَّلَامِ
وَالأَمْرُ بِالْمَعْرُوفِ وَالنَّهْيُ عَنِ الْمُنْكَرِ.

مُتَّفَقٌ عَلَيْهِ

107 Abū Saʿīd al-Khudrī ﷺ reported that the Prophet ﷺ
said: 'Beware of sitting in the streets!' They said: 'O
Allah's Messenger, we have no other place to sit to
talk to each other.' Thereupon Allah's Messenger ﷺ
said: 'If you have no other place to sit, then observe
the rules of the street!' They said: 'What are the
rules of the street, O Allah's Messenger?' He said:
'Lowering the gaze, removing what causes harm,
returning the *salām* and enjoining what is right and
forbidding what is evil.'

Bukhārī, Muslim

عَنْ أَبِي هُرَيْرَةَ ﷺ قَالَ: قَالَ رَسُولُ اللهِ ﷺ: كُلُّ سُلَامَى
مِنَ النَّاسِ عَلَيْهِ صَدَقَةٌ كُلَّ يَوْمٍ تَطْلُعُ فِيهِ الشَّمْسُ: تَعْدِلُ

بَيْنَ اثْنَيْنِ صَدَقَةٌ وتُعينُ الرَّجُلَ في دَابَّتِه فَتَحْمِلُهُ عَلَيْهَا أَوْ
تَرْفَعُ لَهُ عليْهَا مَتَاعَهُ صَدَقَةٌ، وَالكَلِمَةُ الطَّيِّبَةُ صَدَقَةٌ،
وَبِكُلِّ خُطْوَةٍ تَمْشِيهَا إِلَى الصَّلَاةِ صَدَقَةٌ، وَتُميطُ الأَذَى عَنِ
الطَّرِيقِ صَدَقَةٌ.

مُتَّفَقٌ عَلَيْهِ

وَرَوَاهُ مُسْلِمٌ أَيْضًا عَنْ عَائِشَةَ ﷺ قَالَتْ: قَالَ رَسُولُ اللهِ ﷺ:
إِنَّهُ خُلِقَ كُلُّ إِنْسَانٍ مِنْ بَني آدَمَ عَلَى سِتِّينَ وثَلاثَمَائة مِفْصَلٍ،
فَمَنْ كَبَّرَ اللهَ عَزَّ وَجَلَّ وَسَبَّحَ وَاسْتَغْفَرَ وَحَرَّكَ حَجَرًا عَنْ
طَرِيقِ النَّاسِ أَوْ شَوْكَةً أَوْ عَظْمًا عَنْ طَرِيقِ النَّاسِ، أَوْ أَمَرَ
بِمَعْرُوفٍ أَوْ نَهَى عَنْ مُنْكَرٍ عَدَدَ السِّتِّينَ والثَّلاثَمَائة فَإِنَّهُ
يَمْشِي يَوْمَئِذٍ وَقَدْ زَحْزَحَ نَفْسَهُ عَنِ النَّارِ.

108 Abū Huraira ☺ reported that Allah's Messenger ﷺ said: 'Charity[3] is due upon every limb of a human being on each day that the sun rises. To act justly between two (people) is charity. To help a man with his riding beast, or to load his provisions on it or lift them up for him is charity. A good word is charity. Every step going to prayer is charity. Removing from the road what causes harm is charity.'

Bukhārī, Muslim

---

[3] Arabic: *ṣadaqa.*

Muslim also reported from 'Ā'ishah ﷺ who said: Allah's Messenger ﷺ said: 'Every human being from Adam's progeny is created with three hundred and sixty joints. One who declares Allah greatest, praises Allah, declares that there is no god but Allah, glorifies Allah, asks Allah's forgiveness, removes a stone, or a thorn, or a bone from the road where people walk, and enjoins good and forbids evil, to the extent of three hundred and sixty in number, he comes out on the Day (of Judgement) having pulled away his soul from the fire.'

عَنْ أَبِي هُرَيْرَةَ ﵁ أَنَّ رَسُولَ الله ﷺ قَالَ: بَيْنَمَا رَجُلٌ يَمْشِي بِطَرِيقٍ وَجَدَ غُصْنَ شَوْكٍ فَأَخَذَهُ فَشَكَرَ اللهُ لَهُ فَغَفَرَ لَهُ.

رَوَاهُ الْبُخَارِيُّ

109 From Abū Huraira ﵁: Allah's Messenger ﷺ said: 'While a man was walking along, he came across a thorny branch on the way and he removed it. Allah praised him for that and forgave him (of his sins).'

Bukhārī

عَنْ أَبِي ذَرٍّ ﷺ قَـالَ: قَالَ لِي رَسُولُ اللهِ ﷺ: اتَّقِ اللهَ حَيْثُمَا
كُنْـتَ وَأَتْبِـعِ السَّيِّئَةَ الْـحَسَنَةَ تَـمْحُهَا وَخَالِقِ النَّاسَ
بِخُلُقٍ حَسَنٍ.

رَوَاهُ أَحْمَد والتِّرْمِذِيّ

110 Abū Dharr 🙿 reported that Allah's Messenger ﷺ said to him: 'Fear God wherever you are; let an evil deed (be) followed by a good deed so that you blot it out; and be well-behaved towards people.'

Aḥmad, Tirmidhī

عَنْ أَوْسِ بْنِ شُرَحْبِيلَ ﷺ أَنَّهُ سَمِعَ رَسُولَ اللهِ ﷺ يَقُولُ:
مَنْ مَشَى مَعَ ظَالِمٍ لِيُقَوِّيَهُ وَهُـوَ يَعْلَـمُ أَنَّهُ ظَالِمٌ فَقَدْ خَرَجَ
مِنَ الإِسْلَامِ.

رَوَاهُ البَيْهَقِيّ

111 From Aws b. Shuraḥbīl 🙿: he heard Allah's Messenger ﷺ say: 'One who strives to strengthen an oppressor, and knows he is an oppressor, has already left Islam.'

Baihaqī

عَنْ أَبِي سَعِيدِ الْخُدْرِيِّ ﷺ قَالَ: سَمِعتُ رَسُولَ اللهِ ﷺ
يَقُولُ: مَنْ رَأَى مِنْكُمْ مُنْكَرًا فَلْيُغَيِّرْهُ بِيَدِهِ، فَإِنْ لَمْ يَسْتَطِعْ
فَبِلِسَانِهِ، فَإِنْ لَمْ يَسْتَطِعْ فَبِقَلْبِهِ وَذَلِكَ أَضْعَفُ الإِيمَانِ.
رَوَاهُ مُسْلِم

112 From Abu Saʿīd al-Khudrī ﷺ: Allah's Messenger ﷺ
said: 'If one of you sees (something) bad, he should
change it with his hand; and if he is not capable of
that, then with his tongue; and if he is not capable
of that, then (he should detest it) with his heart; and
that is the weakest faith.'

Muslim

⸺⸺⸺

عَنْ أَبِي هُرَيْرَةَ ﷺ أَنَّ رَسُولَ اللهِ ﷺ قَالَ: مَنْ دَعَا إِلَى هُدًى
كَانَ لَهُ مِنَ الْأَجْرِ مِثْلُ أُجُورِ مَنْ تَبِعَهُ لَا يَنْقُصُ ذَلِكَ مِنْ
أُجُورِهِمْ شَيْئًا. وَمَنْ دَعَا إِلَى ضَلَالَةٍ كَانَ عَلَيْهِ مِنَ الْإِثْمِ
مِثْلُ آثَامِ مَنْ تَبِعَهُ لَا يَنْقُصُ ذَلِكَ مِنْ أَوْزَارِهِمْ شَيْئًا.
رَوَاهُ مُسْلِم

113 Abū Huraira ﷺ reported that Allah's Messenger ﷺ
said: 'He who calls to the right guidance, has the
same reward as those who follow him. It will not
lessen their rewards. And he who calls to wrong,

burdens himself with the same sin as the sins of
those who follow him. It will not lessen their sins.'

Muslim

⸺⸺⸻✼⸻⸺⸺

عَنْ أَنَسٍ ﴿رضي الله عنه﴾ أَنَّ رَجُلًا قَالَ لِلنَّبِيِّ ﷺ: أَوْصِنِي. فَقَالَ
النَّبِيُّ ﷺ: خُذِ الأَمْرَ بِالتَّدْبِيرِ فَإِنْ رَأَيْتَ فِي عَاقِبَتِهِ خَيْرًا
فَأَمْضِهِ وَإِنْ خِفْتَ غَيًّا فَأَمْسِكْ.

شَرْحُ السُّنَّةِ

114 From Anas ﷺ: A man said to the Prophet ﷺ: 'Give
me some advice,' and he said: 'Judge each matter by
its disposition. If you see good in its outcome, carry
on with it; but if you fear transgressing the limits set
by Allah, then abstain from it.'

Sharḥ al-Sunna

⸺⸺⸻✼⸻⸺⸺

عَنْ أَبِي هُرَيْرَةَ ﴿رضي الله عنه﴾ قَالَ: قَالَ رَسُولُ اللهِ ﷺ: مِنْ حُسْنِ
إِسْلاَمِ الـمَرْءِ تَرْكُهُ مَا لاَ يَعْنِيهِ.

رَوَاهُ ابْنُ مَاجَه

115 From Abū Huraira ﷺ: Allah's Messenger ﷺ said: 'It
is (part) of the beauty of a man's Islam to leave what
does not concern him.'

Ibn Mājah

عَنْ أَبِي عَبْدِ اللهِ النُّعْمَانِ بْنِ بَشِيرٍ ﴿رضى الله عنهما﴾ قَالَ: سَمِعْتُ رَسُولَ
اللهِ ﷺ يَقُولُ: إِنَّ الحَلَالَ بَيِّنٌ وَإِنَّ الحَرَامَ بَيِّنٌ وَبَيْنَهُمَا أُمُورٌ
مُشْتَبِهَاتٌ لاَ يَعْلَمُهُنَّ كَثِيرٌ مِنَ النَّاسِ، فَمَنِ اتَّقَى الشُّبُهَاتِ
فَقَدِ اسْتَبْرَأَ لِدِينِهِ وَعِرْضِهِ، وَمَنْ وَقَعَ فِي الشُّبُهَاتِ وَقَعَ فِي
الـحَرَامِ كَالرَّاعِي يَرْعَى حَوْلَ الـحِمَى يُوشِكُ أَنْ يَقَعَ فِيهِ.
أَلَا وَإِنَّ لِكُلِّ مَلِكٍ حِمًى، أَلَا وَإِنَّ حِمَى اللهِ مَـحَارِمُـهُ،
أَلَا وَإِنَّ فِي الجَسَدِ مُضْغَةً إِذَا صَلَحَتْ صَلَحَ الجَسَدُ كُلُّهُ
وَإِذَا فَسَـدَتْ فَسَـدَ الجَسَـدُ كُلُّهُ أَلَا وَهِيَ القَلْبُ.

مُتَّفَقٌ عَلَيْهِ

116 Abū 'Abdullāh Nu'mān b. Bashīr ﷺ said that Allah's
Messenger ﷺ said: 'What is lawful is clear and what
is unlawful is (also) clear, but between the two are
doubtful matters of which many people do not know.
He who protects himself from doubtful matters clears
himself in regard to his faith and honour, but he who
falls into doubtful matters is like a shepherd who
grazes (his sheep) around a sanctuary, and (liable)
to graze therein. Surely, every king has a sanctuary.
Surely, the sanctuary of Allah is His prohibitions.
Surely, in the body is a piece of flesh, and if it is
sound, the whole body is sound; and if it is damaged,
the whole body is diseased. Surely, it is the heart.'

Bukhārī, Muslim

عَنِ الحَسَنِ بنِ عَلِيّ ﷺ قَالَ: حَفِظْتُ مِنْ رَسُولِ اللهِ ﷺ:
دَعْ ما يُرِيبُكَ إِلَى مَا لَا يُرِيبُكَ، فَإِنَّ الصِّدْقَ طُمَأْنِينَةٌ وَإِنَّ
الكَذِبَ رِيبَةٌ.

رَوَاهُ أَحْمَد وَالنَّسَائِي وَالتِّرْمِذِيّ

117 Al-Ḥasan b. ʿAli ﷺ said: I preserved the following words from Allah's Messenger ﷺ: 'Leave what you have doubt about for that you have no doubt about; for it is truth that brings peace of mind and it is falsehood that brings doubt.'

Aḥmad, Tirmidhī and Nasāʾī

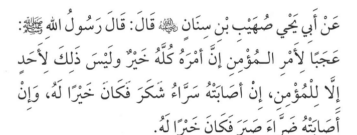

عَنْ أَبِي يَحْيَى صُهَيْب بْنِ سِنَانٍ ﷺ قَالَ: قَالَ رَسُولُ اللهِ ﷺ:
عَجَبًا لِأَمْرِ الـمُؤْمِنِ إِنَّ أَمْرَهُ كُلَّهُ خَيْرٌ وَلَيْسَ ذَلِكَ لِأَحَدٍ
إِلَّا لِلْمُؤْمِنِ، إِنْ أَصَابَتْهُ سَرَّاءُ شَكَرَ فَكَانَ خَيْرًا لَهُ، وَإِنْ
أَصَابَتْهُ ضَرَّاءَ صَبَرَ فَكَانَ خَيْرًا لَهُ.

رَوَاهُ مُسْلِم

118 Abū Yaḥyā Ṣuhaib b. Sinān ﷺ said that Allah's Messenger ﷺ said: 'Wondrous are the believer's affairs. For him there is good in all his affairs, and this is so only for the believer. When something pleasing happens to him, he is grateful, and that is good for him;

and when something displeasing happens to him,
he is enduring, and that is good for him.'

Muslim

———————❧———————

عَنْ أَبِي سَعِيدٍ وَأَبِي هُرَيْرَةَ ﷺ عَنِ النَّبِيِّ ﷺ قَالَ: مَا يُصِيبُ
الْمُسْلِمَ مِنْ نَصَبٍ وَلَا وَصَبٍ وَلَا هَمٍّ وَلَا حَزَنٍ وَلَا أَذًى
وَلَا غَمٍّ حَتَّى الشَّوْكَةُ يُشَاكُهَا إِلَّا كَفَّرَ اللهُ بِهَا مِنْ خَطَايَاهُ.
مُتَّفَقٌ عَلَيْهِ

119 Abū Saʿīd and Abū Huraira ﷺ said that Allah's
Messenger ﷺ said: 'No trouble befalls a Muslim, and
no illness, no sorrow, no grief, no harm, no distress,
not even a thorn pricks him, without Allah expiating
by it (some) of his sins.'

Bukhārī, Muslim

———————❧———————

عَنْ أَبِي هُرَيْرَةَ ﷺ أَنَّ رَسُولَ اللهِ ﷺ قَالَ: لَيْسَ الشَّدِيدُ
بِالصُّرَعَةِ إِنَّمَا الشَّدِيدُ الَّذِي يَمْلِكُ نَفْسَهُ عِنْدَ الْغَضَبِ.
مُتَّفَقٌ عَلَيْهِ

120 From Abū Huraira ﷺ: Allah's Messenger ﷺ said: 'The
strong man is not the one who is strong in wrestling,
but the one who controls himself in anger.'

Bukhārī, Muslim

عَـنْ أَبِي ذَرٍّ ﷺ أَنَّ رَسُـولَ الله ﷺ قَـالَ: إِذَا غَضِـبَ أَحَدُكُمْ وَهُوَ قَائِمٌ فَلْيَجْلِسْ، فَإِنْ ذَهَبَ عنْـهُ الغَضَـبُ وَإِلَّا فَلْيَضْطَجِعْ.

رَوَاهُ أَحْمَد والتِّرْمِذِيّ

121 From Abū Dharr ﷺ: Allah's Messenger ﷺ said: 'When one of you gets angry while he is standing up, he should sit down. Then the anger (will) leave him, and if not, then he should lie down.'

Aḥmad, Tirmidhī

22

Manners of Speech

عَنْ جَابِرٍ ﷺ قَالَ: قَالَ رَسُولُ الله ﷺ: السَّلامُ قَبْلَ الكَلامِ.

رَوَاهُ التِّرْمِذِيّ

122 Jābir ﷺ reported that Allah's Messenger ﷺ said: 'Saying *salām* (comes) before talking.'

Tirmidhī

عَنْ سُفْيَانَ بْنِ عَبْدِ الله الثَّقَفِي ﷺ قَالَ: قُلْتُ: يَا رَسُولَ الله ﷺ حَدِّثْنِي بِأَمْرٍ أَعْتَصِمُ بِهِ. قَالَ: قُلْ رَبِّيَ اللهُ ثُمَّ اسْتَقِمْ. قُلْتُ: يَا رَسُولَ الله مَا أَخْوَفُ مَا تَخَافُ عَلَيَّ؟ فَأَخَذَ بِلِسَانِ نَفْسِهِ ثُمَّ قَالَ: هَذَا!

رَوَاهُ التِّرْمِذِيّ

123 Sufyān b. 'Abdullāh al-Thaqafī ⁕ said: 'I said: "O Allah's Messenger ⁕, tell me something that I should adhere to." He said: "Say: My Lord is Allah; then remain steadfast." I said: "O Allah's Messenger, what do you fear most for me?" Thereupon he took hold of his own tongue and said: "This!"'

Tirmidhī

عَنْ أَبِي هُرَيْرَةَ ﵁ قَالَ: قَالَ رَسُولُ اللهِ ﷺ: مَنْ كَانَ يُؤْمِنُ بِاللهِ وَالْيَوْمِ الْآخِرِ فَلْيَقُلْ خَيْرًا أَوْ لِيَصْمُتْ.

مُتَّفَقٌ عَلَيْه

124 Abū Huraira ⁕ reported that Allah's Messenger ⁕ said: 'He who truly believes in Allah and the Last Day should speak good or keep silent.'

Bukhārī, Muslim

عَنْ عَبْدِ اللهِ بْنِ عَمْرٍو ﵁ قَالَ: قَالَ رَسُولُ اللهِ ﷺ: مَنْ صَمَتَ نَجَا.

رَوَاهُ أَحْمَد والتِّرْمِذِيّ

125 'Abdullāh b. 'Amr ⁕ said that Allah's Messenger ⁕ said: 'He who keeps silent remains safe.'

Aḥmad, Tirmidhī

عَنْ ابْنِ عُمَرَ ﷺ قَالَ: قَالَ رَسُولُ اللهِ ﷺ : لَا تُكْثِـرُوا
الكَلَامَ بِغَيْرِ ذِكْرِ اللهِ، فَإِنَّ كَثْرَةَ الكَلَامِ بِغَيْرِ ذِكْرِ اللهِ قَسْوَةٌ
لِلقَلْبِ وَإِنَّ أَبْعَدَ النَّاسِ مِنَ اللهِ القَلْبُ القَاسِي.

رَوَاهُ التِّرْمِذِيّ

126 Ibn 'Umar ﷺ said that Allah's Messenger ﷺ said:
'Do not talk for long without remembering Allah,
for talking much without remembering Allah is
hardness of the heart. The most distant among man
from Allah is one with a hardened heart.'

Tirmidhī

عَـنْ أَبِي هُـرَيْـرَةَ ﷺ أَنَّ رَسُــولَ اللهِ ﷺ قَـالَ: أَتَـدْرُونَ
مَا الْغِيبَةُ؟ قَالُوا: اللهُ وَرَسُولُهُ أَعْلَمُ! قَالَ: ذِكْرُكَ أَخَـاكَ
بِمَـا يَكْرَهُ. قِيلَ: أَفَرَأَيْتَ إِنْ كَانَ فِي أَخِي مَا أَقُولُ؟ قَالَ: إِنْ
كَانَ فِيهِ مَا تَقُولُ فَقَدِ اغْتَبْتَهُ وَإِنْ لَمْ يَكُنْ فِيهِ فَقَدْ بَهَتَّهُ.

رَوَاهُ مُسْلِم

127 Abū Huraira ﷺ reported that Allah's Messenger ﷺ
said: 'Do you know backbiting?' They said: 'Allah
and His Messenger know best.' He said: '(When)
you speak about your brother, what he would dislike

it is backbiting.' Someone said: 'What if my brother is as I say?' He said: 'If he is as you say, you have been backbiting; and if he is not as you say, you have slandered him.'

Muslim

وَعَنْ عَبْدِ اللهِ بْنِ عَمْرِو بْنِ الْعَاصِ ﷺ قَالَ: لَمْ يَكُنْ رَسُولَ اللهِ ﷺ فَاحِشًا وَلَا مُتَفَحِّشًا.

مُتَّفَقٌ عَلَيْه

128 'Abdullāh b. 'Amr b. al-'Āṣ ﷺ said that Allah's Messenger ﷺ never used obscene talk nor did he listen to it.

Bukhārī, Muslim

عَنْ عِيَّاضِ بْنِ حِمَارٍ الْمُجَاشِعِيّ ﷺ أَنَّ رَسُولَ اللهِ ﷺ خَطَبَهُمْ فَقَالَ: إِنَّ اللهَ أَوْحَى إِلَيَّ أَنْ تَوَاضَعُوا وَلَا يَفْخَرَ أَحَدٌ عَلَى أَحَدٍ وَلَا يَبْغِيَ أَحَدٌ عَلَى أَحَدٍ.

رَوَاهُ مُسْلِم

129 From ʿIyāḍ b. Ḥimār al-Mujāshiʿī ﷺ: Allah's Messenger ﷺ said: 'Allah has revealed to me: "You should be humble so that no-one boasts over his neighbour nor anyone oppresses his neighbour."'

Muslim

عَنْ بَهْزِ بْنِ حَكِيمٍ عَنْ أَبِيهِ عَنْ جَدِّهِ ﷺ قَالَ: سَمِعْتُ رَسُولَ اللهِ ﷺ يَقُولُ: وَيْلٌ لِـمَنْ يُحَدِّثُ فَيَكْذِبُ لِيُضْحِكَ بِهِ الْقَوْمَ، وَيْلٌ لَهُ، وَيْلٌ لَهُ، وَيْلٌ لَهُ .

رَوَاهُ أَحْمَد وَالتِّرْمِذِيّ

130 From Bahz b. Ḥakīm, from his father, from his grandfather ﷺ: Allah's Messenger ﷺ said: 'Woe to him who tells lies to make people laugh – Woe to him, woe to him, woe to him!'

Aḥmad, Tirmidhī

عَنْ سُفْيَانَ بْنِ أَسَدٍ الْـحَضْرَمِيّ ﷺ قَالَ: سَـمِعْتُ رَسُولَ اللهِ ﷺ يَقُولُ: كَبُرَتْ خِيَانَةً أَنْ تُحَدِّثَ أَخَاكَ حَدِيثًا هُوَ لَكَ مُصَدِّقٌ وَأَنْتَ لَهُ كَاذِبٌ.

رَوَاهُ أَبُو دَاوُد

131 From Sufyān b. Asad al-Ḥaḍramī ﷺ: I heard Allah's Messenger ﷺ say: 'It is great treachery that you tell your brother something he accepts as truth from you, but you are lying.'

Abū Dāwūd

عَنْ عَبْدَ اللهِ بْنِ مَسْعُودٍ ﷺ قَـالَ: قَالَ رَسُولُ اللهِ ﷺ: لَا يُبَلِّغُنِي أَحَدٌ مِنْ أَصْحَابِي عَنْ أَحَدٍ شَيْئًا، فَإِنِّي أُحِبُّ أَنْ أَخْرُجَ إِلَيْكُمْ وَأَنَا سَلِيمُ الصَّدْرِ.

رَوَاهُ أَبُو دَاوُد

132 From 'Abdullāh b. Mas'ūd ﷺ: Allah's Messenger ﷺ said: 'None of my companions should tell me anything about anyone, for I like to meet (any one) of you with a clean heart.'

Abū Dāwūd

عَنْ عَائِشَةَ ﷺ قَالَتْ: كَانَ كَلَامُ رَسُولِ اللهِ ﷺ كَلَامًا فَصْلًا يَفْهَمُهُ كُلُّ مَنْ يَسْمَعُهُ.

رَوَاهُ أَبُو دَاوُد

133 'Ā'ishah ﷺ said that the speech of Allah's Messenger ﷺ was clear and distinct such that all those who listened to him understood him.

Abū Dāwūd

23

Ẓuhr Prayer

عَنْ جَابِرِ بْنِ سَمُرَةَ ﷺ قَالَ: كَانَ النَّبِيُّ ﷺ يُصَلِّي الظُّهَرَ
إِذَا دَحَضَتِ الشَّمْسُ.

رَوَاهُ ابْنُ مَاجَه

134 From Jābir b. Samura ﷺ: The Prophet ﷺ used to pray *ẓuhr* when the sun lost strength.

Ibn Mājah

عَنْ عَبْدِ اللهِ بْنِ السَّائِبِ ﷺ قَالَ: كَانَ رَسُولُ اللهِ ﷺ يُصَلِّي
أَرْبَعًا بَعْدَ أَنْ تَزُولَ الشَّمْسُ قَبْلَ الظُّهْرِ. وقال: إِنَّهَا سَاعَةٌ
تُفْتَحُ فِيهَا أَبْوَابُ السَّمَاءِ فَأُحِبُّ أَنْ يَصْعَدَ لِي فِيهَا
عَمَلٌ صَالِحٌ.

رَوَاهُ التَّرْمِذِيّ

135 'Abdullāh b. Sā'ib ⬥ said that Allah's Messenger ﷺ used to pray four *(rak'as)* after the sun declined, before the noon prayer, and he said: 'This is the hour when the gates of heaven are opened, and I wish that a righteous deed of mine might rise up (to heaven) during this (hour).'

Tirmidhī

❀ 24 ❀

Living with People

عَنْ عَبْدِ الله بْنِ عُمَرَ ﷺ قَـالَ: قَـالَ رَسُولُ الله ﷺ:
اَلْـمُسْلِمُ الَّذِي يُخَالِطُ النَّاسَ وَيَصْبِرُ عَلَى أَذَاهُمْ خَيْرٌ مِنْ
الَّذِي لَا يُخَالِطُ النَّاسَ وَلَا يَصْبِرُ عَلَى أَذَاهُمْ.

رَوَاهُ التِّرْمِذِيّ

136 From 'Abdullāh b. 'Umar ﷺ: The Prophet ﷺ said:
'The Muslim who meets with people and endures
any harm they may do is better than he who does
not mix with them and does not endure any harm
they may do.'

Tirmidhī

━━━━━━━━━━━

عَنْ عَبْدِ الله بْنِ عَمْرِو بْنِ الْعَاصِ ﷺ أَنَّ رَسُولَ الله ﷺ
قَالَ: الرَّاحِمُونَ يَرْحَمُهُمُ الرَّحْمَنُ، ارْحَمُوا مَنْ فِي الأَرْضِ
يَرْحَمْكُمْ مَنْ فِي السَّمَاءِ.

رَوَاهُ أَبُو دَاوُدَ وَالتِّرْمِذِيُّ

137 'Abdullāh b. 'Amr b. al-'Āṣ ﷺ reported that Allah's Messenger ﷺ said: 'The Merciful One shows mercy to those who are themselves merciful (to others). So show mercy to whatever is on earth, then He who is in heaven will show mercy to you.'

Abū Dāwūd, Tirmidhī

عَنْ جَـابِرِ بْنِ عَبْدِ اللهِ ﷺ قَـالَ: قَالَ رَسُـولُ اللهِ ﷺ:
لَا يَرْحَمُ اللهُ مَنْ لَا يَرْحَمُ النَّاسَ.

مُتَّفَقٌ عَلَيْه

138 Jābir b. 'Abdullāh ﷺ said that Allah's Messenger ﷺ said: 'Allah is not merciful to him who is not merciful to people.'

Bukhārī, Muslim

عَنْ أَبِي هُرَيْرَةَ ﷺ قَالَ: قَالَ رَسُولُ اللهِ ﷺ: مَنْ لَمْ يَشْكُرِ
النَّاسَ لَمْ يَشْكُرِ اللهَ.

رَوَاهُ أَحْمَد وَأَبُو دَاوُدَ وَالتِّرْمِذِيُّ

139 From Abū Huraira ﷺ: Allah's Messenger ﷺ said: 'He who does not thank people does not thank Allah.'

Aḥmad, Abū Dāwūd, Tirmidhī

عَنْ أُسَـامَةَ بْنِ زَيْدٍ ﷺ قَالَ: قَالَ رَسُولُ اللهِ ﷺ: مَنْ صُنِعَ إِلَيْهِ مَعْرُوفٌ فَقَـالَ لِفَاعِلِـهِ جَـزَاكَ اللهُ خَـيْـرًا فَقَـدْ أَبْلَغَ فِي الثَّنَاءِ.

رَوَاهُ التَّرْمِذِيُّ

140 Usāma b. Zaid ﷺ said: Allah's Messenger ﷺ said: 'When someone has had good done to him and says to the doer "May Allah reward you,"[1] he has done the utmost in praise.'

Tirmidhī

عَنْ أَنَسٍ ﷺ قَالَ: قَالَ رَسُولُ اللهِ ﷺ: وَالَّذِي نَفْسِي بِيَدِهِ لَا يُؤْمِنُ عَبْدٌ حَتَّى يُحِبَّ لِأَخِيهِ مَا يُحِبُّ لِنَفْسِهِ .

مُتَّفَقٌ عَلَيْهِ

141 From Anas ﷺ: Allah's Messenger ﷺ said: 'By Him in Whose hand is my soul, a servant (of Allah) does not believe (truly) until he likes for his brother what he likes for himself.'

Bukhārī, Muslim

---

[1] Arabic: *jazāka aIlāhU khairan*

عَنْ الْـمِقْدَام بْنِ مَعْدِي كَرِب ﷺ عَنِ النَّبِيِّ ﷺ قَالَ:
إِذَا أَحَـبَّ الرَّجُـلُ أَخَاهُ فَلْيُخْبِرْهُ أَنَّهُ يُحِبُّهُ.
رَوَاهُ أَبُو دَاوُدَ وَالتِّرْمِذِيُّ

142 From al-Miqdām b. Ma'dī Karib ﷺ: The Prophet ﷺ said: 'When a man loves his brother he should tell him that he loves him.'

Abū Dāwūd, Tirmidhī

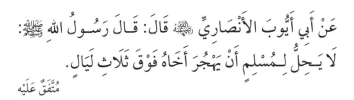

عَنْ أَبِي أَيُّوبَ الأَنْصَارِيِّ ﷺ قَالَ: قَالَ رَسُـولُ الله ﷺ:
لَا يَـحِلُّ لِمُسْلِمٍ أَنْ يَهْجُرَ أَخَاهُ فَوْقَ ثَلَاثِ لَيَالٍ.
مُتَّفَقٌ عَلَيْهِ

143 From Abū Ayyūb al-Anṣārī ﷺ: Allah's Messenger ﷺ said: 'It is not right for a man to forsake his brother for more than three days.'

Bukhārī, Muslim

عَنْ جَابِرٍ ﷺ عَنْ رَسُولِ اللهِ ﷺ أَنَّهُ قَالَ: مَنِ اعْتَذَرَ إِلَى
أَخِيهِ فَلَمْ يَعْذُرْهُ، أَوْ لَمْ يَقْبَلْ عُذْرَهُ، كَانَ عَلَيْهِ مِثْلُ خَطِيئَةِ
صَاحِبِ مَكْسٍ.

رَوَاهُ البَيْهَقِيّ

144 Jābir ﷺ reported that Allah's Messenger ﷺ said: 'If one makes excuses to his brother, but he does not excuse him, or accept his apology, he is as sinful as one who takes an unjust tax.'

Baihaqī

25

Sitting Together

عَنْ أَبِي هُرَيْرَةَ ﷺ قَالَ: قَالَ رَسُولُ الله ﷺ: إِذَا انْتَهَى أَحَدُكُمْ إِلَى الْمَجْلِسِ فَلْيُسَلِّمْ، فَإِذَا أَرَادَ أَنْ يَقُومَ فَلْيُسَلِّمْ، فَلَيْسَ الأُولَى بِأَحَقَّ مِنَ الآخِرَةِ.

رَوَاهُ أَبُو دَاوُد

145 Abū Huraira ﷺ reported that Allah's Messenger ﷺ said: 'When one of you arrives where people are seated, he should say *salām* to them. And when he wishes to leave, he should say *salām* to them. The former is as appropriate as the latter.'

Abū Dāwūd

عَنْ أَبِي أُمَامَةَ ﷺ قَالَ: خَرَجَ عَلَيْنَا رَسُولُ الله ﷺ يَتَوَكَّأُ عَلَى عَصًا فَقُمْنَا إِلَيْهِ فَقَالَ: لَا تَقُومُوا كَمَا تَقُومُ الأَعَاجِمُ بَعْضُهَا لِبَعْضٍ.

رَوَاهُ أَبُو دَاوُد

146 From Abū Umāma ﷺ: Allah's Messenger ﷺ came out leaning on a stick and we stood up. He said: 'Do not stand up as the foreigners stand up exalting each other therewith.'

Abū Dāwūd

عَنِ ابْنِ عُمَرَ ﷺ عَنِ النَّبِيِّ ﷺ قَالَ: لَا يُقِيمَنَّ أَحَدُكُمْ رَجُلاً مِنْ مَجْلِسِهِ ثُمَّ يَجْلِسُ فِيهِ، وَلَكِنْ تَوَسَّعُوا وتَفَسَّحُوا. مُتَّفَقٌ عَلَيْهِ

147 From Ibn 'Umar ﷺ: The Prophet ﷺ said: 'No man shall make another man get up from where he is sitting and then sit himself there, rather you should make space and room!'

Bukhārī, Muslim

عَنْ عَمْرِو بْنِ شُعَيْبٍ عَنْ أَبِيهِ عَنْ جَدِّهِ ﷺ أَنَّ رَسُولَ اللهِ ﷺ قَالَ: لَا يَحِلُّ لِرَجُلٍ أَنْ يُفَرِّقَ بَيْنَ اثْنَيْنِ إِلَّا بِإِذْنِهِمَا. رَوَاهُ أَبُو دَاوُد

148 From 'Amr b. Shu'aib, from his father, from his grandfather ﷺ: Allah's Messenger ﷺ said: 'Do not sit between two men without the permission of both of them.'

Abū Dāwūd

عَنْ جَابِرِ بن سَمُرَةَ ﴿رضي الله عنه﴾ قَالَ: جَاءَ رَسُولُ اللهِ ﷺ وَأَصْحَابُهُ جُلُوسٌ، فَقَالَ: مَالِي أَرَاكُمْ عِزِينَ؟

رَوَاهُ أَبُو دَاوُد

149 From Jābir b. Samura ﴿رضي الله عنه﴾: Allah's Messenger ﷺ came and his companions were seated. He said: 'Why do I see you in separate groups?'

Abū Dāwūd

عَنْ عَبْدِ اللهِ بن مَسْعُودٍ ﴿رضي الله عنه﴾ قَالَ: قَالَ رَسُولُ اللهِ ﷺ: إِذَا كُنْتُمْ ثَلَاثَةً فَلَا يَتَنَاجَى اثْنَانِ دُونَ الآخَرِ مِنْ أَجْلِ أَنْ يُحْزِنَه.

مُتَّفَقٌ عَلَيْه

150 'Abdullāh b. Mas'ūd ﴿رضي الله عنه﴾ said: Allah's Messenger ﷺ said: 'When you are three together, two (of you) must not converse privately without the third until you are in the company of other people, because it makes him sad.'

Bukhārī, Muslim

عَنْ جَـابِرِ بْنِ عَبْـدِ اللهِ ﷺ قَـالَ : قَالَ رَسُـولُ اللهِ ﷺ:
إِذَا حَدَّثَ الرَّجُلُ بِحَدِيثٍ ثُمَّ الْتَفَتَ فَهِيَ أَمَانَةٌ.

رَوَاهُ التِّرْمِذِيُّ

151 From Jābir b. 'Abdullāh ﷺ: The Prophet ﷺ said:
'When a man talks of something and leaves, then
(what he said) is a trust.'

Tirmidhī

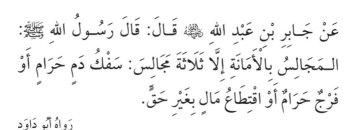

عَنْ جَـابِرِ بْنِ عَبْدِ اللهِ ﷺ قَالَ: قَالَ رَسُـولُ اللهِ ﷺ:
الْـمَجَالِسُ بِالْأَمَانَةِ إِلَّا ثَلَاثَةَ مَجَالِسَ: سَفْكُ دَمٍ حَرَامٍ أَوْ
فَرْجٌ حَرَامٌ أَوِ اقْتِطَاعُ مَالٍ بِغَيْرِ حَقٍّ.

رَوَاهُ أَبُو دَاوَد

152 Jābir b. 'Abdullāh ﷺ said: Allah's Messenger ﷺ
said: 'Meetings are like trusts, except three kinds
of meeting: for shedding prohibited blood, or for
committing fornication or for taking property
unlawfully.'

Abū Dāwūd

عَنْ أَبِي هُرَيْرَةَ ﷺ قَالَ: قَالَ رَسُولُ الله ﷺ: مَنْ جَلَسَ فِي مَجْلِسٍ فَكَثُرَ فِيهِ لَغَطُهُ فَقَالَ قَبْلَ أَنْ يَقُومَ مِنْ مَجْلِسِهِ ذَلِكَ: سُبْحَانَكَ اللَّهُمَّ وَبِحَمْدِكَ، أَشْـهَدُ أَنْ لَا إِلَـهَ إِلَّا أَنْتَ أَسْتَغْفِرُكَ وَأَتُوبُ إِلَيْكَ، إِلَّا غُفِرَ لَـهُ مَا كَانَ فِي مَجْلِسِهِ ذَلِكَ.

رَوَاهُ التِّرْمِذِيُّ

153 Abū Huraira ﷺ reported that Allah's Messenger ﷺ said: 'He who sits in a company where there is much idle talk, and before he gets up from his place says: "Glory be to You, O Allah, and praise be to You. I witness that there is no god but You. I seek Your forgiveness and I turn to You in repentance,"[1] then his having been in that company is forgiven.'

Tirmidhī

عَنِ ابْنِ عَبَّاسٍ ﷺ أَنَّ رَسُولَ الله ﷺ قَالَ: لَا يَخْلُوَنَّ رَجُلٌ بِامْرَأَةٍ إِلَّا مَعَ ذِي مَحْرَمٍ.

مُتَّفَقٌ عَلَيْهِ

---

[1] Arabic: *Subḥānaka Allahumma wa bi-ḥamdik. Ashhadu an lā ilāha illā anta, astaghfiruka wa atūbu ilaik.*

154 From Ibn 'Abbās : Allah's Messenger said: 'None of you should be alone with a woman unless she is with a *maḥram*.'[2]

Bukhārī, Muslim

---

[2] A near relative who cannot be married according to Islamic law.

26

'Aṣr **Prayer**

عَنْ عَائِشَةَ ﷺ قَالَتْ: صَلَّى النَّبِيُّ ﷺ العَصْرَ والشَّمْسُ في
حُجْرَتِي لَمْ يُظْهِرْهَا الفَيْءُ بَعْدُ.

رَوَاهُ ابن مَاجَه

155 ‘Āʾishah ﷺ said: The Prophet ﷺ prayed ‘Aṣr and the sun was shining in my room. The afternoon shade was not yet apparent.

Ibn Mājah

⟨⟨⟨⟩⟩⟩

عَنِ ابْنِ عُمَرَ ﷺ عَنْ رَسُولَ الله ﷺ قَالَ: إِنَّ الَّذِي تَفُوتُهُ
صَلاةُ العَصْرِ كَأَنَّمَا وُتِرَ أَهْلُهُ وَمَالُهُ.

مُتَّفَقٌ عَلَيْه

156 Ibn ʿUmar ﷺ reported that Allah's Messenger ﷺ said: 'He who misses the ‘Aṣr prayer is like one who has lost (some of) his family and his property.'

Bukhārī, Muslim

✵ 27 ✵

Visiting

عَنْ مُعَاذِ بنِ جَبَلٍ ﷺ قَالَ: سَـمِعْتُ رَسُولَ الله ﷺ
يَقُولُ: قال اللهُ تَبَارَكَ وتَعَالَى: وَجَبَتْ مَحَبَّتِي لِلْمُتَحَابِّينَ فِيَّ
والـمُتَجَالِسِينَ فِيَّ والـمُتَزَاوِرِينَ فِيَّ والـمُتَبَاذِلِينَ فِيَّ.
رَوَاهُ مَالِكٌ

وفي رِوَايَةِ التِّرْمِذِيّ: يَقُولُ اللهُ عَزَّ وجَلَّ: الـمُتَحَابُّونَ فِي
جَلالِي لَـهُمْ مَنَابِرُ مِنْ نُورٍ يَغْبِطُهُمْ النَّبِيُّونَ والشُّهَدَاءُ.

157 Muʿādh b. Jabal ﷺ said that he heard Allah's Messenger ﷺ say: 'Allah the Exalted said: "My love is due to those who love each other for My sake, who sit with each other for My sake, who visit one another for My sake, who spend on each other for My sake."'

Mālik

In Tirmidhī's report, it says: 'Allah the Exalted said: "Those who love each other for My glory, for them will be pulpits of light, and the prophets and martyrs will deem them fortunate."'

عَنْ أَبِي مُوسَى الأَشْعَرِيِّ ﷺ قَالَ: قَالَ رَسُولُ اللهِ ﷺ:
الاِسْتِئْذَانُ ثَلَاثٌ، فَإِنْ أُذِنَ لَكَ وَإِلَّا فَارْجِعْ.

مُتَّفَقٌ عَلَيْهِ

158 Abū Mūsā al-Ash'arī ﷺ reported that Allah's Messenger ﷺ said: 'Permission to enter is to be asked three times. If permission is given to you, then enter, otherwise leave.'

Bukhārī, Muslim

عَنْ كَلَدَةَ بْنِ حَنْبَلٍ ﷺ قَالَ: دَخَلْتُ عَلَى النَّبِيِّ ﷺ وَلَمْ
أُسَلِّمْ وَلَمْ أَسْتَأْذِنْ فَقَالَ النَّبِيُّ ﷺ: ارْجِعْ فَقُلْ: السَّلَامُ
عَلَيْكُمْ، أَأَدْخُلُ؟

رَوَاهُ التِّرْمِذِيُّ وَأَبُو دَاوُد

159 Kalada b. Ḥanbal ﷺ said: I arrived at Allah's Messenger's ﷺ and entered and did not say *salām* and did not ask permission. Thereupon Allah's Messenger said: 'Go back and say: "Peace be upon you, may I enter?"'

Tirmidhī, Abū Dāwūd

عَنْ جَابِرِ بْنِ عَبْدِ الله ﴿رضي الله عنه﴾ قَالَ: أَتَيْتُ النَّبِيَّ ﷺ فَدَقَقْتُ
البَابَ فَقَالَ: مَنْ هَذَا؟ فَقُلْتُ: أَنَا! فَقَالَ: أَنَا! أَنَا!
كَأَنَّهُ كَرِهَهَا.

160 Jābir b. ʿAbdullāh ﴿رضي الله عنه﴾ said: 'I came to the Prophet ﷺ and knocked at the door and he asked: "Who is there?" I said: "I." He said: "I? I?" as if he disliked it.'

Bukhārī, Muslim

عَنْ قَتَادَةَ ﴿رضي الله عنه﴾ قَالَ: قَالَ النَّبِيُّ ﷺ: إِذَا دَخَلْتُمْ بَيْتًا فَسَلِّمُوا
عَلَى أَهْلِهِ، وَإِذَا خَرَجْتُمْ فَأَوْدِعُوا أَهْلَهُ بِسَلامٍ.

رَوَاهُ البَيْهَقِيّ

161 Qatāda ﴿رضي الله عنه﴾ reported that the Prophet ﷺ said: 'When you enter a house, say *salām* to its occupants, and when you go out, leave its occupants with saying *salām*.'

Baihaqī

28

Visiting the Sick

عَنْ أَبِي مُوسَى ﷺ قَالَ: قَالَ رَسُولُ اللهِ ﷺ: عُودُوا الْـمَرِيضَ وَأَطْعِمُوا الْجَائِعَ وَفُكُّوا الْعَانِي.

رَوَاهُ الْبُخَارِيّ

162 Abū Mūsā ﷺ reported that Allah's Messenger ﷺ said: 'Visit the sick, feed the hungry and free the captives.'

Bukhārī

عَنْ أَبِي هُرَيْرَةَ ﷺ قَالَ: قَالَ رَسُولُ اللهِ ﷺ: مَنْ عَادَ مَرِيضًا أَوْ زَارَ لَهُ أَخًا نَادَى لَهُ مُنَادٍ مِنَ السَّمَاءِ: أَنْ طِبْتَ وَطَابَ مَمْشَاكَ وَتَبَوَّأْتَ مِنَ الْـجَنَّةِ مَنْزِلًا.

رَوَاهُ التِّرْمِذِيّ

163 From Abū Huraira 📿: Allah's Messenger ﷺ said: 'One who visits a sick person, or visits a brother of his for the sake of Allah, a caller calls him (saying): "May you be well, and may your passage be well, and may you occupy a place in paradise."'

Tirmidhī

29

Ṣadaqa

عَنْ أَنَسٍ ﷺ قَالَ: قَالَ رَسُولُ الله ﷺ: إِنَّ الصَّدَقَةَ لَتُطْفِئُ
غَضَبَ الرَّبِ وتَدْفَعُ مِيتَةَ السُّوءِ.

رَوَاهُ التِّرْمِذِيّ

164 From Anas ﷺ: Allah's Messenger ﷺ said: '*Ṣadaqa* extinguishes the Lord's anger and repels evil death.'

Tirmidhī

عَنْ أَسْمَاءَ بِنْتِ أَبِي بَكْرٍ ﷺ أَنَّهَا جَاءَتْ إِلَى النَّبِيِّ ﷺ فَقَالَ:
لا تُوعِي فَيُوعِيَ الله عَلَيْكِ، ارْضَخِي مَا اسْتَطَعْتِ.

رَوَاهُ البُخَارِيّ

165 From Asmā' bint Abī Bakr ﷺ: She came to the Prophet ﷺ and he said: 'Do not withhold or Allah withholds from you. Give away whatever you can afford.'

Bukhārī

عَنْ أَنَسَ بْنَ مَالِكٍ ﵁ قَـالَ: قَالَ رَسُولُ اللهِ ﷺ: أَفْضَلُ الصَّدَقَةِ أَنْ تُشْبِعَ كَبِدًا جَائِعًا.

رَوَاهُ البَيْهَقِيّ

166 From Anas b. Mālik ﵁: Allah's Messenger ﷺ said: 'The most excellent *Ṣadaqa* is that you feed a hungry stomach.'

Baihaqī

———— ❀ ————

عَنْ عَدِيِّ بْنِ حَاتِمٍ ﵁ قَالَ: قَالَ رَسُولُ اللهِ ﷺ: اتَّقُوا النَّارَ وَلَوْ بِشِقِّ تَمْرَةٍ، فَإِنْ لَمْ تَجِدُوا فَبِكَلِمَةٍ طَيِّبَةٍ.

رَوَاهُ مُسْلِم

167 'Adiyy b. Ḥātim ﵁ reported that Allah's Messenger ﷺ said: 'Protect yourself against the Fire, even if it be only by (giving) a piece of date, and if one cannot even fulfil this, then by (saying) a good word.'

Muslim

———— ❀ ————

عَنْ أَبِي ذَرٍّ ﵁ قَالَ: قَالَ لِي رَسُولُ اللهِ ﷺ: لَا تَحْقِرَنَّ مِنَ المَعْرُوفِ شَيْئًا وَلَوْ أَنْ تَلْقَى أَخَاكَ بِوَجْهٍ طَلِيقٍ.

مُتَّفَقٌ عَلَيْهِ

168 From Abū Dharr ⬡: Allah's Messenger ﷺ said: 'Do not look down on anything good, even if it is meeting your brother with a cheerful face.'

Muslim

30

Gifts

عَنْ أَبِي هُرَيْرَةَ ﷺ عَنِ النَّبِيِّ ﷺ قَالَ: تَهَادُوْا فَإِنَّ الْـهَدِيَّةَ تُذْهِبُ وَحْرَ الصَّدْرِ.

رَوَاهُ التِّرْمِذِيّ

169 From Abū Huraira ﷺ: The Prophet ﷺ said: 'Give gifts to one another, for a gift removes rancour from the breast.'

Tirmidhī

عَنْ عَائِشَةَ ﷺ قَالَتْ: كَانَ رَسُولُ اللهِ ﷺ يَقْبَلُ الْـهَدِيَّةَ وَيُثِيبُ عَلَيْهَا.

رَوَاهُ الْبُخَارِي

170 From 'Ā'ishah ﷺ: Allah's Messenger ﷺ used to accept gifts and used to give (gifts) in return.

Bukhārī

عَنْ أَبِي هُرَيْرَةَ ﷺ قَالَ: قَالَ رَسُولُ اللهِ ﷺ: مَنْ عُرِضَ عَلَيْهِ رَيْحَانٌ فَلَا يَرُدَّهُ فَإِنَّهُ خَفِيفُ الـمَحْمَلِ طَيِّبُ الرِّيحِ.
رَوَاهُ مُسْلِم

171 Abū Huraira ﷺ reported that Allah's Messenger ﷺ said: 'He to whom perfume is given should not refuse it, for it is light in weight and good in smell.'

Muslim

31

Maghrib Prayer

عَنْ سَلَمَةَ ﴿رَضِيَ اللهُ عَنهُ﴾ قَالَ: كُنَّا نُصَلِّي مَعَ النَّبِيِّ ﷺ الْمَغْرِبَ إِذَا تَوَارَتْ بِالْحِجَابِ.

رَوَاهُ مُسْلِمٌ

172 Salama ﴿رضي الله عنه﴾ said: 'We used to pray the *maghrib* prayer with the Prophet ﷺ when (the sun) disappeared into its place of seclusion.'

Bukhārī

32

Neighbours

عَنْ عَبْدِ اللهِ بْنِ عَمْرَ ﴿رضي﴾ قَالَ: قَالَ رَسُولُ اللهِ ﷺ: خَيْرُ
الْأَصْحَابِ عِنْدَ اللهِ خَيْرُهُمْ لِصَاحِبِهِ، وَخَيْرُ الْجِيرَانِ عِنْدَ
اللهِ خَيْرُهُمْ لِجَارِهِ.

رَوَاهُ التِّرْمِذِي

173   'Abdullāh b. 'Umar ﷺ reported that Allah's Messenger ﷺ said: 'The best companion in the sight of Allah the Exalted is he who behaves best to his companions, and the best neighbour in the sight of Allah the Exalted is he who behaves best to his neighbour.'

Tirmidhī

عَنْ أَبِي هُرَيْرَةَ ﵁ أَنَّ النَّبِيَّ ﷺ قَالَ: وَاللهِ لَا يُؤْمِنُ! وَ اللهِ
لَا يُؤْمِنُ! وَاللهِ لَا يُؤْمِنُ! قِيلَ: وَمَنْ يَا رَسُولَ اللهِ؟ قَالَ:
الَّذِي لَا يَأْمَنُ جَارُهُ بَوَايِقَهُ.

مُتَّفَقٌ عَلَيْهِ

وفي روايةِ مُسْلِمٍ: لَايَدْخُلُ الجَنَّةَ مَنْ لا يَأْمَنُ جَارُهُ بَوَائِقَهُ.

174 Abū Huraira ﵁ reported that Allah's Messenger ﷺ
said: 'By Allah, he does not (truly) believe! By Allah,
he does not (truly) believe! By Allah, he does not
(truly) believe!' Someone asked: 'Who, O Allah's
Messenger?' He said: 'He whose neighbour is not
safe from his mischief.'

Bukhārī, Muslim

And in Muslim's report, it says: 'He will not enter
paradise whose neighbour is not safe from his
mischief.'

عَنْ أَبِي ذَرٍّ ﵁ قَالَ: قَالَ رَسُولُ اللهِ ﷺ: إِذَا طَبَخْتَ مَرَقَةً
فَأَكْثِرْ مَاءَهَا وَتَعَاهَدْ جِيرَانَكَ.

رَوَاهُ مُسْلِم

175 From Abū Dharr ﵁ said: Allah's Messenger ﷺ said:
'When you cook soup add more water, remembering
your neighbours.'

Muslim

33

Guests

عَنْ أَبِي شُرَيْحِ الْـخُزَاعِي رَضِيَ اللهُ عنه قَالَ : سَمِعْتُ رَسُولَ اللهِ ﷺ
يَقُولُ: مَنْ كَانَ يُؤْمِنُ بِاللهِ وَالْيَوْمِ الآخِرِ فَلْيُكْرِمْ ضَيْفَهُ
جَائِزَتَهُ. قَالُوا: وَمَا جَائِزَتُهُ يَا رَسُولَ اللهِ؟ قَالَ: يَوْمٌ وَلَيْلَةٌ،
وَالضِّيَافَةُ ثَلَاثَةُ أَيَّامٍ فَمَـا كَانَ وَرَاءَ ذَلِكَ فَهْوَ صَدَقَةٌ عَلَيْهِ.
مُتَّفَقٌ عَلَيْهِ

176 Abū Shuraiḥ al-Khuzāʿī ﷺ said: 'I heard Allah's
Messenger ﷺ say: "He who believes in Allah and
the Last Day should honour his guest according
to his right." People asked: "And what is his right,
Messenger of Allah?" He said: "A day and a night,
and hospitality for three days. And beyond that is
ṣadaqa."'

Bukhārī, Muslim

عَنْ أَبِي هُرَيْرَةَ ﷺ قَالَ: قَالَ رَسُولُ اللهِ ﷺ: مِنَ السُّنَّةِ أَنْ
يَخْرُجَ الرَّجُلُ مَعَ ضَيْفِهِ إِلَى بَابِ الدَّارِ.

رَوَاهُ ابْنُ مَاجَه

177 From Abū Huraira ﷺ: Allah's Messenger ﷺ said: 'It
is (part) of the *Sunnah* that a man accompanies his
guest to the door of the house.'

Ibn Mājah

34

The Family

عَنْ أَنَسِ بْنِ مَالِكٍ ﷺ قَالَ: قَالَ لِي رَسُولُ الله ﷺ: يَا بُنَيَّ!
إِذَا دَخَلْتَ عَلَى أَهْلِكَ فَسَـلِّمْ يَكُنْ بَرَكَةً عَلَيْكَ وَعَلَى
أَهْـلِ بَيْتِكَ.

رَوَاهُ التِّرْمِذِيّ

178 Anas b. Mālik ؓ said: Allah's Messenger ﷺ said:
'O my son, when you enter to where your family is,
say *salām.* It is a blessing on you and on the people
of your house.'

Tirmidhī

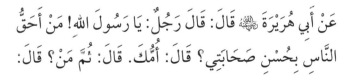

عَنْ أَبِي هُرَيْرَةَ ؓ قَالَ: قَالَ رَجُلٌ: يَا رَسُولَ الله! مَنْ أَحَقُّ
النَّاسِ بِحُسْنِ صَحَابَتِي؟ قَالَ: أُمُّكَ. قَالَ: ثُمَّ مَنْ؟ قَالَ:

ثُمَّ أُمَّكَ. قَالَ: ثُمَّ مَنْ؟ قَالَ: ثُمَّ أُمَّكَ. قَالَ: ثُمَّ مَنْ؟ قَالَ:
ثُمَّ أَبُوكَ.

مُتَّفَقٌ عَلَيْه

179 Abū Huraira ؇ said: A man came to Allah's Messenger ﷺ and said: 'O Allah's Messenger, who of mankind is most entitled to the best of my companionship?' He said: 'Your mother.' He said: 'Then who?' He said: 'Your mother.' He said: 'Then who?' He said: 'Your mother.' He said: 'Then who?' He said: 'Your father.'

Bukhārī, Muslim

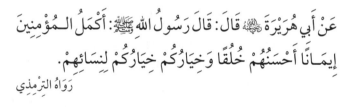

عَنْ أَبِي هُرَيْرَةَ ؇ قَالَ: قَالَ رَسُولُ اللهِ ﷺ: أَكْمَلُ الْـمُؤْمِنِينَ
إِيمَانًا أَحْسَنُهُمْ خُلُقًا وَخِيَارُكُمْ خِيَارُكُمْ لِنِسَائِهِمْ.

رَوَاهُ التِّرْمِذِي

180 Abū Huraira ؇ reported that Allah's Messenger ﷺ said: 'The most perfect of believers is the best of you in character; and the best of you are those among you who are best to their wives.'

Tirmidhī

عَنْ أَبِي مَسْعُودٍ البَدْرِيّ ﷺ عَنِ النَّبِيِّ ﷺ أَنَّه قَالَ: إِذَا أَنْفَقَ
الرَّجُلُ عَلَى أَهْلِهِ نَفَقَةً وَهُوَ يَحْتَسِبُهَا، كَانَتْ لَهُ صَدَقَةً.
مُتَّفَقٌ عَلَيْه

181 From Abū Mas'ūd al-Badrī ﷺ: Allah's Messenger ﷺ
said: 'When a man spends to support his family
hoping (for Allah's reward) it is counted for him as
ṣadaqa.'

Bukhārī, Muslim

عَنْ عَبْدِ اللهِ بْنِ عَمْرٍو ﷺ قَالَ: قَالَ رَسُولُ اللهِ ﷺ: لَيْسَ
مِنَّا مَنْ لَمْ يَرْحَمْ صَغِيرَنَا وَيَعْرِفْ شَرَفَ كَبِيرِنا.
رَوَاهُ أَبُو داوُد والتِّرْمِذِيّ

182 From 'Abdullāh b. 'Amr ﷺ: Allah's Messenger ﷺ
said: 'He is not of us who has no compassion for our
little ones and does not honour our old ones.'

Abū Dāwūd, Tirmidhī

عَنْ عَائِشَةَ ﷺ قَالَتْ: أَتَى النَّبِيَّ ﷺ أُنَاسٌ مِنَ الْعَرَب
فَقَالَ لَهُ رَجُلٌ مِنْهُمْ: يَا رَسُولَ اللهِ! أَتُقَبِّلُونَ الصِّبْيَانَ؟

فَوَاللهِ مَا نُقَبِّلُهُمْ. فَقَالَ رَسُولُ اللهِ ﷺ: أَوَ أَمْلِكُ إِنْ كَانَ اللهُ قَدْ نَزَعَ مِنْ قَلْبِكَ الرَّحْمَةَ.

مُتَّفَقٌ عَلَيْهِ

183 'Ā'ishah ؓ said: A desert Arab came to the Prophet ﷺ and said: 'Do you kiss children? We do not kiss them.' The Prophet said: 'What can I do for you if Allah has taken away mercy from your heart?'

Bukhārī, Muslim

———— ❦ ————

عَنْ عَمْرِو بْنِ شُعَيْبٍ عَنْ أَبِيهِ عَنْ جَدِّهِ ؓ قَالَ: قَالَ رَسُولُ اللهِ ﷺ: مُرُوا أَوْلادَكُمْ بِالصَّلاةِ وَهُمْ أَبْنَاءُ سَبْعِ سِنِينَ وَاضْرِبُوهُمْ عَلَيْهَا وَهُمْ أَبْنَاءُ عَشْرٍ وَفَرِّقُوا بَيْنَهُمْ فِي الْمَضَاجِعِ.

رَوَاهُ أَبُو دَاوُد

184 From 'Amr b. Shu'aib, from his father, from his grandfather ؓ, who said: Allah's Messenger ﷺ said: 'Command your children to pray when they are seven years of age, and punish them (if they do not say them) when they are ten years of age, and separate their beds (at that age).'

Abū Dāwūd

عَنْ أَبِي هُرَيْرَةَ ﴿رضي الله عنه﴾ قَالَ: قَالَ رَسُولُ الله ﷺ: خَيْرُ بَيْتٍ فِي الـمُسْلِمِينَ بَيْتٌ فِيهِ يَتِيمٌ يُحْسَنُ إِلَيْهِ، وَشَرُّ بَيْتٍ فِي الـمُسْلِمِينَ بَيْتٌ فِيهِ يَتِيمٌ يُسَاءُ إِلَيْهِ.

رَوَاهُ ابْنُ مَاجَه

185 From Abū Huraira ﷺ: Allah's Messenger ﷺ said: 'The best house among Muslims is the house in which an orphan is well treated and the worst house among the Muslims is the house in which an orphan is badly treated.'

Ibn Mājah

عَنِ الأَسْوَدِ ﴿رضي الله عنه﴾ قَالَ: سَأَلْتُ عَائِشَةَ ﴿رضي الله عنها﴾: مَا كَانَ النَّبِيُّ ﷺ يَصْنَعُ فِي أَهْلِهِ؟ قَالَتْ: كَانَ فِي مِهْنَةِ أَهْلِهِ فَإِذَا حَضَرَتْ الصَّلَاةُ قَامَ إِلَى الصَّلَاةِ.

رَوَاهُ الْبُخَارِيّ

186 Al-Aswad ﷺ said: I asked 'Ā'ishah ﷺ: 'What did the Prophet ﷺ used to do in his house?' She said: 'He used to work for his family, that is, serve his family, and when prayer (time) came, he went out for prayer.'

Bukhārī

35

Teaching and Learning

عَنْ ابْنِ عُمَرَ ﷺ عَنِ النَّبِيِّ ﷺ أَنَّهُ قَالَ: كُلُّكُمْ رَاعٍ وَكُلُّكُمْ مَسْـُوُولٌ عَنْ رَعِيَّتِهِ، فَالأَمِيرُ رَاعٍ وَالرَّجُـلُ رَاعٍ عَلَى أَهْلِ بَيْتِهِ، وَالـمَرْأَةُ رَاعِيَةٌ عَلَى بَيْتِ زَوْجِها وَوَلَدِهِ فَكُلُّكُمْ رَاعٍ وَكُلُّكُمْ مَسْئُولٌ عَنْ رَعِيَّتِهِ.

مُتَّفَقٌ عَلَيْهِ

187 lbn 'Umar ﷺ reported that Allah's Messenger ﷺ said: 'Each of you is a guardian, and each of you will be asked about your guardianship. The leader is a guardian, and the man is a guardian over the people of his house, and the woman is a guardian over her husband's house and children. So each of you is a guardian, and each of you will be asked about your guardianship.'

Bukhārī, Muslim

عَنْ عُثْمَانَ بْنِ عَفَّانَ ﷺ قَالَ: قَالَ رَسُولُ الله ﷺ: خَيْرُكُمْ
مَنْ تَعَلَّمَ الْقُرْآنَ وَعَلَّمَهُ.

رَوَاهُ الْبُخَارِيّ

188 'Uthmān b. 'Affān ﷺ said: Allah's Messenger ﷺ said: 'The best of you is he who has learnt the Qur'ān and then taught it.'

Bukhārī

عَنْ أَبِي هُرَيْرَةَ ﷺ قَالَ: قَالَ رَسُولُ الله ﷺ: مَا اجْتَمَعَ
قَوْمٌ فِي بَيْتٍ مِنْ بُيُوتِ الله يَتْلُونَ كِتَابَ الله وَيَتَدَارَسُونَهُ
بَيْنَهُمْ إِلَّا نَزَلَتْ عَلَيْهِمُ السَّكِينَةُ وَغَشِيَتْهُمُ الرَّحْمَةُ وَحَفَّتْهُمُ
الْمَلَائِكَةُ وَذَكَرَهُمُ الله فِيمَنْ عِنْدَهُ.

رَوَاهُ مُسْلِم

189 Abū Huraira ﷺ reported that Allah's Messenger ﷺ said: 'Never do people gather in one of the houses of Allah to recite the book of Allah and teach it to each other without Allah's peace coming down upon them, mercy covering them, angels surrounding them and Allah speaking of them to those who are with Him.'

Muslim

عَنْ مَالِكِ بْنِ الْحُوَيْرِثِ ﴿رضي الله عنه﴾ قَالَ: قَالَ لَنَا النَّبِيُّ ﷺ:
ارْجِعُوا إِلَى أَهْلِكُمْ فَعَلِّمُوهُمْ.

رَوَاهُ الْبُخَارِيّ

190
Mālik b. Ḥuwairith ﷺ reported that the Prophet ﷺ said to us: 'Go back to your people and teach them.'
Bukhārī

عَنْ أَنَسٍ ﴿رضي الله عنه﴾ عَنِ النَّبِيِّ ﷺ قَالَ: يَسِّرُوا وَلَا تُعَسِّرُوا
وَبَشِّرُوا وَلَا تُنَفِّرُوا.

مُتَّفَقٌ عَلَيْه

191
From Anas ﷺ: The Prophet ﷺ said: 'Make things easy, and do not make them difficult, and give good tidings and do not make people run away.'
Bukhārī

36

'Ishā' **Prayer**

عَنْ أَبِي هُرَيْرَةَ ﷺ قَالَ: قَالَ رَسُولُ اللهِ ﷺ: لَيْسَ صَلاةٌ
أَثْقَلَ عَلَى الـمُنَافِقِينَ مِنْ صَلاةِ الفَجْرِ والعِشَاءِ، ولوْ
يَعْلَمُونَ مَا فِيهِمَا لأَتَوْهُمَا ولَوْ حَبْوًا.

مُتَّفَقٌ عَلَيْه

192 Abū Huraira ﷺ reported that Allah's Messenger ﷺ
said: 'No prayer is more burdensome to the hypo-
crites than the *fajr* prayer and the *'ishā'* prayer, but if
they knew what (blessings) lie in them they would
certainly come for them, even if they had to crawl.'

Bukhārī, Muslim

37

Witr **Prayer**

عَنْ عَلِيٍّ ﷺ قَالَ: قَالَ رَسُولُ اللهِ ﷺ: إِنَّ اللهَ وِتْرٌ يُحِبُّ الْوِتْرَ، فَأَوْتِرُوا يَا أَهْلَ الْقُرْآنِ .

رَوَاهُ التِّرْمِذِيّ وأَبُو داوُد

193 From 'Alī ﷺ: Allah's Messenger ﷺ said: 'Allah is single,[1] He loves what is single, therefore do the *witr*, O you people of the Qur'ān.'

Tirmidhī, Abū Dāwūd

عَنْ جَابِرٍ ﷺ قَالَ: قَالَ رَسُولُ اللهِ ﷺ: مَنْ خَافَ أَنْ لَا يَقُومَ مِنْ آخِرِ اللَّيْلِ فَلْيُوتِرْ أَوَّلَهُ، وَمَنْ طَمِعَ أَنْ يَقُومَ آخِرَهُ فَلْيُوتِرْ آخِرَ اللَّيْلِ فَإِنَّ صَلَاةَ آخِرِ اللَّيْلِ مَشْهُودَةٌ وَذَلِكَ أَفْضَلُ .

رَوَاهُ مُسْلِم

---

[1] Arabic: *witr*.

194 From Jābir : Allah's Messenger ﷺ said: 'He who fears that he will not get up in the latter part of the night should do the *witr* in the first part of it; and he who eagerly wishes to get up in the latter part of it should do the *witr* then, for prayer in the latter part of the night is witnessed and that is more excellent.'

Muslim

✤ 38 ✤

Intercourse

عَنِ ابْنِ عَبَّاسٍ ﵁ عن النَّبِيِّ ﷺ أنَّهُ قَالَ: لَوْ أَنَّ أَحَدَكُمْ
إِذَا أَتَى أَهْلَهُ قَالَ: بِسْمِ اللهِ، اللَّهُمَّ جَنِّبْنَا الشَّيْطَانَ وَجَنِّبِ
الشَّيْطَانَ مَا رَزَقْتَنَا، فَقَضَى بَيْنَهُمَا وَلَدٌ، لَمْ يَضُرُّهُ.
مُتَّفَقٌ عليه

195 From Ibn 'Abbās ﵁: The Prophet ﷺ said: 'When one
of you goes unto his wife and says: "In the name of
Allah – O Allah ward off the *Shaiṭān* from us, and
ward off the *Shaiṭān* from what You bestow on us!"[1]
and if a child is destined for them, the *Shaiṭān* will
not harm it.'

Bukhārī

---

[1] Arabic: *Bismi-llāh. Allahumma jannibnā-l-Shaiṭāna wa jannibi-
l-Shaiṭāna mā razaqtanā.*

عَنْ عَائِشَةَ ﵂ أَنَّهَا قَالَتْ: كَانَ رَسُولُ اللهِ ﷺ إِذَا أَرَادَ أَنْ يَنَامَ وَهُوَ جُنُبٌ تَوَضَّأَ وُضُوءَهُ لِلصَّلاةِ قَبْلَ أَنْ يَنَامَ.
رَوَاهُ الْبُخَارِيّ

196 'Ā'ishah ﵂ said: the Prophet ﷺ when he wanted to sleep while he was *junub*,[2] used to wash his private parts and make ablution for prayer before he slept.

Bukhārī

---

[2] Being ritually impure after sexual intercourse.

39

Sleep

عن جابرٍ ﷺ قَالَ: قَالَ رَسُولُ الله ﷺ: إِذَا كَانَ جُنْحُ اللَّيْلِ
أَوْ أَمْسَيْتُمْ فَكُفُّوا صِبْيَانَكُمْ فَإِنَّ الشَّيْطَانَ يَنْتَشِرُ حِينَئِذٍ.
فَإِذَا ذَهَبَ سَاعَةٌ مِنَ اللَّيْلِ فَخَلُّوهُمْ، وَأَغْلِقُوا الأَبْوَابَ
وَاذْكُرُوا اسْمَ الله فَإِنَّ الشَّيْطَانَ لَا يَفْتَحُ بَابًا مُغْلَقًا، وَأَوْكُوا
قِرَبَكُمْ وَاذْكُرُوا اسْمَ الله، وَخَمِّرُوا آنِيَتَكُمْ وَاذْكُرُوا اسْمَ الله،
وَلَوْ أَنْ تَعْرِضُوا عَلَيْهَا شَيْئًا وَأَطْفِئُوا مَصَابِيحَكُمْ .
رَوَاهُ مُسْلِم

197 Jābir ﷺ said that Allah's Messenger ﷺ said: 'When
the darkness of the night or evening (comes), then
keep in your children, for the *Shaiṭān* is then out.
And when an hour of the night has gone, then let
them go and close the doors, and invoke the name
of Allah, for the *Shaiṭān* does not open a closed door,
and tie up your waterskins and invoke the name of
Allah, and cover your vessels and invoke the name

of Allah, even when you put something on them, and put out your lights.'

Muslim

عَنْ البَرَاءِ بنِ عَازِبٍ ﷺ قَالَ: كَانَ رَسُولُ اللهِ ﷺ إذَا آوَى إلى فِرَاشِهِ نَامَ عَلَى شَقِّهِ الأيمَنِ ثُمَّ قَالَ: اللَّهُمَّ أَسْلَمْتُ نَفْسي إلَيْكَ ووَجَّهْتُ وَجْهي إلَيْكَ وَفَوَّضْتُ أمْرِي إلَيْكَ وَأَلْـجَأْتُ ظَهْرِي إلَيْكَ، رَغْبَـةً ورَهْبَـةً إلَيْكَ، لَا مَلْجَأَ ولَا مَنْجَا مِنْكَ إلَّا إلَيْكَ. آمَنْتُ بِكِتَابِكَ الّذي أَنْزَلْتَ، ونَبِيِّكَ الّذي أَرْسَلْتَ.

رَوَاهُ البُخَارِيّ

198 Barā' b. 'Āzib said ﷺ: Allah's Messenger ﷺ, when going to bed, used to lie down on his right side and then say: 'O Allah, I surrender myself to You and turn my face towards You, and entrust myself to You, and seek protection in You, longing for You and fearing You; there is no protection and no escape from You except with You. I believe in Your book, which You sent down, and Your Prophet, whom You sent.'[1]

Bukhārī

---

[1] Arabic: *Allahumma aslamtu nafsī ilaika wa wajjahtu wajhī ilaika wa fawwaḍtu amrī ilaika wa alja'tu ẓahrī ilaika raghbatan wa rahbatan ilaika lā malja'a walā manjā minka illā ilaika āmantu bi-kitābika al-ladhī anzalta wa nabiyyika al-ladhī arsalta.*

✻ 40 ✻

Remembrance of Allah

عَنْ عَبْدِ اللهِ بْنِ خُبَيْبٍ عَنْ أَبِيهِ ﷺ قَالَ: قَـالَ لِي رَسُـولُ
اللهِ ﷺ: قُـلْ: قُـلْ هُـوَ اللهُ أَحَدٌ وَالْمُعَوِّذَتَيْنِ حِينَ تُمْسِي
وَتُصْبِحُ ثَلَاثَ مَرَّاتٍ تَكْفِيكَ مِنْ كُلِّ شَيْءٍ.

رَوَاهُ أَبُو دَاوُد وَالتِّرْمِذِيّ

199 From 'Abdullāh b. Khubaib, from his father ﷺ who reported that Allah's Messenger ﷺ said to him: 'Read *Qul huwa Llāhu aḥad*,[1] and the two last chapters[2] (of the Qur'ān) evening and morning three times. This is sufficient for you in all respects.'

Abū Dāwūd, Tirmidhī

---

[1] *Sūrah* 112
[2] *Sūrahs* 113 and 114.

عَنْ جَابِرٍ ﷺ قَالَ: سَمِعْتُ رَسُولَ اللهِ ﷺ يَقُولُ: أَفْضَلُ الذِّكْرِ لَا إِلَهَ إِلَّا اللهُ.

رَوَاهُ التِّرْمِذِيّ

200 Jābir ﷺ said: I heard Allah's Messenger ﷺ say: 'The best remembrance (of Allah) is *lā ilāha illā Llāhu*.'[3]

Tirmidhī

---

[3] 'There is no god except Allah.'